HOW TO BUY &

In this Series

BUY & RUN A SHOP

A Practical Guide to Successful Retailing

Iain Maitland

Second Edition

How To Books

By the same author

Franchising: A Practical Guide for Franchisors and Franchisees
The Business Planner
How to Recruit
The Barclays' Guide to Managing Staff for the Small Business
Running a Successful Advertising Campaign

Author's dedication
To Tracey, Michael and Sophie

British Library cataloguing-in-publication data
A catalogue record for this book is available
from the British Library

© 1992 by Iain Maitland

First published in 1989. Fully revised and re-set second edition published
1992 by How To Books Ltd, Plymbridge House, Estover Road, Plymouth
PL6 7PZ, United Kingdom. Tel: Plymouth (0752) 735251/695745. Fax:
(0752) 695699. Telex: 45635.

Typeset by PDQ Typesetting, Stoke-on-Trent
Printed and bound by The Cromwell Press, Broughton Gifford, Melksham

Preface

This fully revised, second edition is written for anyone—young or old, male or female, employed or unemployed—who is interested in becoming a self-employed retailer, either by starting a shop from scratch or through purchasing an existing outlet. Everything you need to know is set out here, in a clear, step-by-step way.

'Introducing Retailing' considers choosing your trade, evaluating yourself, making preliminary decisions and seeking advice. 'Raising Finance' shows you how to identify sources of finance, recognise types of finance, compose a business plan and approach a lender for funds.

'Starting Up' discusses searching for the right opportunity, taking vacant premises, buying a going concern, fitting the property, stocking the shelves, insuring your business and opening the doors to the public for the first time. 'Keeping Records' then tells you how to do the books, prepare and analyse accounts, tackle tax, handle VAT and National Insurance.

'Marketing Yourself' studies the importance of conducting research, pricing products and services properly, promoting your shop and selling goods on a face-to-face basis. 'Employing Staff' goes on to explain how to hire employees, manage a workforce, motivate a team and fire employees.

'Understanding Law' details the main terms of the leading employment, health and safety and consumer protection laws. It also lists the questions most often asked by retailers and suggests answers. 'Facing the Future' looks ahead to when you will be ready to expand, and indicates how to review the past so that you can succeed again and again in the coming years. Written in a friendly, down-to-earth style, and supported by illustrative material, checklists, further reading, useful addresses and a glossary, this hands-on guide to successful retailing is essential reading for all would-be shopkeepers. It will help you to turn your dreams into realities by highlighting what—and what not—to do every step of the way.

Iain Maitland

Contents

List of illustrations

1
Introducing Retailing

Begin by spending some time thinking about shopkeeping and what you want to do. You should consider:

- choosing your trade
- evaluating yourself
- making preliminary decisions
- seeking advice.

CHOOSING YOUR TRADE

You probably already know which type of shop you want to buy and run, perhaps a newsagent's, stationer's, bookstore or bedding centre. Whatever it is, it will really pay you to discover all you can about that particular trade before going any further with your hopes and plans: its particular advantages and disadvantages, likely sales, costs, profits and so on. You need to find out everything and anything if you are to make informed, correct decisions about your future. Talk endlessly to retailers, suppliers, agents and the trade association (see page 21). Continually read business and trade journals and books (see page 141). Work in the type of outlet you wish to start, even as an unpaid assistant if necessary, to soak up the pros and cons of that trade, and retailing in general.

Shopkeeping, whether in a bakery, sweetshop or toystore, differs greatly from how people on the other side of the counter fondly imagine it to be. In theory there are many positive aspects: you are your own boss and are able to choose which hours, days and weeks to work; it is an almost idyllic existence with little to do except sit behind a counter each day reading a book with one hand whilst raking in money with the other; all you need to do is to smile sweetly at customers, charge outrageous prices and you'll be sitting on a little goldmine. This is what outsiders naïvely seem to think.

What are the disadvantages of shopkeeping?

In reality there are innumerable negative aspects which people do not always recognise. Whatever the trade, the hours are long—far lengthier than most employees ever have to work. You may have to tidy the shop, attend to petty cash and deal with the post before opening the doors on time in the mornings. You will need to be on call all day, including tea and lunch breaks, to help customers and assist employees with any problems and/or complaints that they cannot handle. Cashing up, completing books and records and delivering goods to customers could take up most of your evenings. On Sundays you might have to collect stock from suppliers, or nowadays open the shop to compete with multiple retailers. Make no mistake about retailing, it is almost certain to be a seven days a week, 52 weeks a year slog, especially at first.

The physical demands

Shopkeeping is physically demanding as well, in most trades. Goods may need to be made by you, often requiring painstaking or possibly backbreaking, sweaty work. Stock deliveries may have to be unloaded, lifted and carried into the storeroom or onto the shopfloor, unpacked and stacked on shelves. You might have to maintain and/or repair items for your customers in order to make a living. Other chores around the property—securing doors and windows, painting and decorating, plumbing and so forth—may need to be handled by you too. Without doubt, shopkeeping is a hard taskmaster.

Stress factors

Even worse, shopkeeping is mentally stressful. As a self-employed retailer, your wage packet depends wholly on your turnover, costs and profits. You will worry every day about whether you will take enough money to pay the business and household bills. You have to be forever vigilant to keep costs down and profits up, buying and selling at the right prices, paying invoices and chasing payments at the correct times. Get it wrong and there will be less or even no profit left for you to live on. Through all of this you need to keep smiling, staying cheerful for your customers. Don't forget you're at the sharp end too: suppliers, employees and customers with problems will come to you, expecting their difficulties to be solved immediately. Retailing is a pressure cooker way of life.

The financial risk

To top everything, shopkeeping is financially risky, especially in recessionary times. Although statistics vary, depending on your viewpoint, it is undeniable that most small, independent shops close down within a few years of opening their doors. Some retailers find themselves just not suited to this lifestyle, or perhaps they make too many errors, such as insufficient funding, a poorly chosen business, too much slow-selling stock, inadequate control systems and so on. Others do everything properly but find circumstances are against them; perhaps a nationally known store opens nearby, or a recession takes hold of the market. Do not be under any illusions, even if your approach is perfect the unforgiving statistics suggest you are as likely to fail as to succeed.

EVALUATING YOURSELF

If you are determined to press ahead, first consider all the qualities required to be a successful shopkeeper and whether or not you possess them in abundance. You need a mix of self-confidence and willpower to get a business off the ground and keep it going year after year. You have to believe in your own talents and abilities and need the conviction, after listening to all of the arguments for and against, to keep on despite the problems which you will encounter.

Your temperament is important: a cool and analytical person will always do better than a rash hothead. Losing your temper with stonewalling bank managers, slow-to-deliver suppliers and confused customers will be counterproductive. Suddenly deciding to carry a new range of goods, hold a sale or drop an existing service without fully appraising the likely pros and cons of different courses of action is a recipe for impending setbacks or out-and-out disaster.

Some knowledge and experience of your proposed trade, and retailing in general, are essential if you plan to start a business from scratch and very desirable if you are going to purchase an existing concern. The complete novice who has never worked in the chosen trade nor stood behind a counter in his or her life has almost no chance of success. There is much to learn in so little time, and the pitfalls are many and varied.

The winning retailer has to be a good all-rounder, able enough to spot a suitable site and quality premises, charm a bank manager, suppliers and customers, keep accurate books and records, advertise his or her business and so on. Too often, retailers have one predominant skill to the exclusion of others. They may make a first class product but not possess the social skills required to sell it, or buy popular goods from wholesalers but under- or overprice or mistreat them. You ought to be a Jack or Jacquie of all trades—and master of them all too.

Should you have a family, you must have their wholehearted support. If not, forget your plans and stick to a 9 to 5 job. Your partner and any children should be prepared to see less of you, to help out in the shop as and when needed (often without pay) and to have fewer evenings and days out, as well as more infrequent holidays. Greater financial constraints will be imposed on them: spending money on household items, clothes, toys and treats will have to be much reduced for the foreseeable future.

Good health, both physical and mental, is another essential ingredient in the make-up of the winning retailer. You need SAS toughness to handle long hours and heavy lifting. Colds, coughs, flu, migraines, bad backs and other ailments are for wimps. However you feel, you need to keep on working. Mental toughness—to cut up rough when necessary and to smile through financial adversity—is just as important. You cannot afford to ignore bank managers' letters, have a funny turn or reach for the bottle during bad times.

Why do you want to be a shopkeeper?

Think too about your motives for going into the retail trade, to make sure that they are truly appropriate. Ideally, you should almost burn inside to be your own boss, knowing you have what it takes—temperament, skills and so forth—to make a go of your down-to-earth ideas. It should be a lifelong ambition. A brooding sense of feeling unfulfilled in a job, the fear or reality of unemployment, a surplus of redundancy money to spend, a desire to do 'something': all these are inappropriate reasons which smack of uncertainty and half-heartedness. These are not the factors that should be driving you into shopkeeping.

Then consider your goals, being certain that they are wholly realistic. Earning a reasonable living, equal to or slightly above the average industrial wage, for a hard day's graft is achievable. 'Having a good time', 'taking things easy', 'having a bit of a laugh' and 'making a fortune'—all of which are real quotes from would-be retailers—reveal attitudes that are likely to lead to abject failure.

MAKING PRELIMINARY DECISIONS

Convinced that retailing, your chosen trade and you are all well matched, you then need to make varous decisions about your future. You must think about the pros and cons of starting a business **from**

scratch, purchasing a **going concern** and taking a **franchise**. You should also contemplate the benefits and drawbacks of trading as a **sole proprietor**, in a **partnership** or as a **franchisee**.

Starting from scratch

The idea of creating a brand new concern from your own thoughts and in your own image is an immensely appealing one. Shut your eyes and you can almost see it, beautifully placed next to Marks and Spencer in a custom built unit which is full of attractive stock and happy customers thrusting £10 notes into your hands. Open your eyes to reality, though. Launching a venture can be successful—especially if it is done by a very experienced retailer—but is an extremely hazardous course for a novice to undertake. You need to find both a suitable property and premises—an almost nightmarish task. You have to fit out the property, but don't know how to. You must obtain stock from suppliers, but are unsure what stock and which suppliers to use. There are hundreds of decisions to make every step of the way. One error—such as a bad site or a poor supplier—and you could be in deep trouble.

Purchasing a going concern

Buying and running an existing business may be a wiser option. If it is trading successfully, this suggests that it is well located in quality premises and is selling the correct stock to a sufficient number of customers. Most—even all—of the teething problems of a new firm will have been dealt with, meaning less risks for you. Receiving advice from the owner, you can take over an established shop with customers and money coming in from the first day. Of course, an existing business will be costly, into five figures in most instances. Also, winning formulae are hard to change without alienating and losing customers. Moving up or down market is easy to talk about, sometimes impossible and always difficult to achieve.

Taking a franchise

Franchising involves one party (the 'franchisor') developing a winning business which is then licensed (or 'franchised') to another person (the 'franchisee') to start and run an identikit concern in a certain area for a given period. In its favour, a franchise offers an established track record so that the chances of an identical business succeeding are that much higher. Having a well known name may make it easier to raise funds, obtain supplies and draw in customers. Also, the franchisor is ever present—at the beginning and on a continuing basis—to tell and show you what to do. Thus, the hopefully correct decisions can be made quickly so that the business is not slowed up or harmed in any way. For the inexperienced prospective retailer, a franchise may be the ideal compromise between starting from scratch and buying an established unit.

Taking a franchise can be costly, often as expensive as an up and running concern (which in many ways is what it is). An initial fee for the franchisor's know-how, normal start-up expenses and ongoing payments of perhaps ten per cent of turnover for the franchisor's continuing help will need to be paid. In addition, you will have to operate to a set format and will not be allowed to make changes without the franchisor's permission, which is unlikely to be given. You are also highly dependent upon the franchisor and other franchisees in the network for your success; if the franchisor doesn't assist you as promised, or fellow franchisees give the network a bad name, your business could suffer or even be destroyed.

Going it alone

You may want to work alone as a sole proprietor, perhaps employing part time staff or your family and friends for odd jobs as and when necessary. For many entrepreneurs, this is the most appropriate trading format as you control and run the business, making decisions on your own. You do not have to refer or answer to anyone but yourself. Your affairs are private and confidential (except for your statutory obligations such as submitting accounts to the Inland Revenue for income tax assessment purposes). It is quite easy to start trading with few legal formalities (see page 73).

There are several disadvantages which you need to think about too. You probably have limited funds of your own to buy and run a shop and will find it difficult to raise additional sums, especially in a recessionary climate. You may also lack the necessary breadth of skills, knowledge and experience to maximise the success of your firm (and the advice of outsiders, however well intentioned, is not always accurate). If you are sick or ill, the shop may have to close temporarily. Most worrying of all, a sole trader is personally responsible for each and every debt incurred. This means that the people and businesses to whom you owe monies can force you to sell both your business and personal assets to meet the debts.

Getting together

To remove many of the disadvantages of going it alone, consider getting together with one or more associates to form a partnership.

Some benefits are the same as for sole traders; in particular, business affairs remain private matters and trading can quickly commence. In addition, capital and borrowing capabilities are increased as is expertise, with each partner concentrating on tasks for which they are best suited. One may deal with book-keeping and accounts, another with marketing and publicity. Reasonable holidays and time off can be arranged, with partners covering for each other's absences and illnesses.

There are of course drawbacks as well. Many partnerships make a successful start but flounder later on when some partners work harder than others and everyone wants to progress in different directions. Also, you will still be personally liable for debts, and could in the last resort lose your home and personal possessions. Even worse, partners are **jointly and severally responsible** for the partnership's debts, which means that an untrustworthy or foolish partner can run up debts in the partnership's name which you are then equally liable to settle.

Should you wish to form a partnership, be cautious of linking up with friends or relatives as many people are inclined to do. A partnership is a commercial marriage which often ends in divorce; you don't want it to destroy your family and/or friendships too. Look for like-minded business people with distinct yet complementary skills to your own. Consult a solicitor (see page 21) to draw up a partnership agreement which sets a framework which you may work within. A checklist of its suggested contents is shown here.

Partnership agreement checklist
1 The partners' names and addresses.
2 The partnership's name and address.
3 Its trade or profession.
4 The partner's capital investments.
5 Their responsibilities for investing additional funds.
6 The ratios and methods of sharing profits and losses.
7 The partners' management and work responsibilities.
8 Their salaries and drawings.
9 The holiday and sickness arrangements.
10 The partnership's length.
11 The terms and conditions of withdrawing from the partnership.
12 The terms and conditions of selling shares of the partnership.
13 The grounds for the dissolution of the partnership.
14 The procedures relating to the permanent illness, retirement or death of the partners.

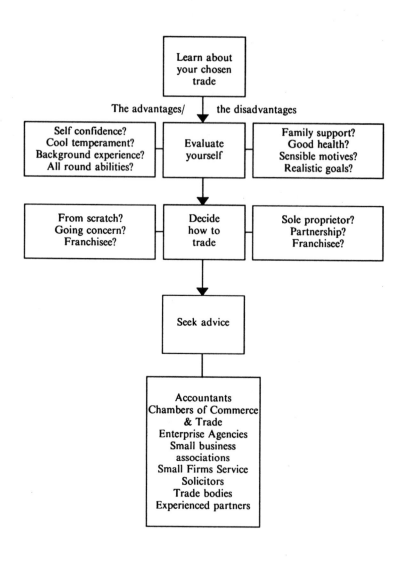

Fig 1. How do you prepare to become a retailer?

As a franchisee
Being a franchisee, either alone or in a partnership with other people, could appeal to you. If it does, you must (as always) compare the advantages and disadvantages for you, according to your circumstances. Also think about the type of personality required to become a winning franchisee, which may be slightly different from other retailing. You need to be independent enough to make day-to-day decisions yet sufficiently disciplined to do as the franchisor suggests; ambitious to expand but capable of working in tandem and so on. Contact the trade organisation, The British Franchise Association, for advice (see page 145). Read everything that you can lay your hands on (refer to page 141).

SEEKING ADVICE

If you want to be a winner, you have to be prepared to seek and listen to advice at all times. All of the following can assist you on both an initial and continuing basis:

- accountants
- chambers of commerce or trade
- enterprise agencies
- small business associations
- the Small Firms Service
- solicitors
- trade bodies
- other experienced individuals and organisations

Using accountants
You ought to employ and regularly refer to an accountant as he or she can help you with so many financial matters:

- identifying sources of finance
- matching the right types of finance to your needs
- composing a business plan
- approaching a lender
- doing the books
- preparing and analysing accounts
- tackling tax

The list is almost endless.

Select one by asking the two professional associations—The

Chartered Association of Certified Accountants and the Institute of Chartered Accountants (page 145)—to send you details of their local members. Visit each of them to discuss your requirements, their range of services and fees. Use your chosen accountant as a sounding board in the early days and for complex work (such as tax topics) later on. Question excessive bills and be ready to switch your allegiance if you are unhappy.

Chambers of commerce or trade
These are scattered across the country, in villages, towns and cities. Organised and run by local traders—which usually means that one or two enthusiasts do all the work whilst others remain apathetic—they can offer general and specific guidance on local issues. As long as the chamber isn't administered by a rival, you can expect assistance on subjects such as

- choosing a location and shop property
- finding fixtures and fittings
- stocking the shelves
- conducting research
- understanding employment and legal matters.

A broad spectrum of advice is available. Contact the Association of British Chambers of Commerce and the National Chamber of Trade for appropriate addresses and phone numbers (see page 145).

Using enterprise agencies
Most of the 300 or so enterprise agencies in the United Kingdom are administered by a charity known as Business in the Community (see page 145) and provide free advisory and counselling services on all small business issues. Chat to them about anything whenever you are puzzled or worried. If their counsellors cannot personally resolve your concerns, they can pass you over to other experts as necessary.

Small business associations
Innumerable organisations have been established to help small businesses to survive through good and bad times. Bodies such as the Alliance of Independent Retailers, the Alliance of Small Firms and Self-Employed People Limited, the National Association of Shop-keepers, the National Federation of Self-Employed and Small Businesses and the Small Businesses Bureau (see page 145) all offer assorted benefits to their members, including a broad-based advisory

service. It may be worth joining such an organisation for useful back-up support.

If you employ under 20 staff in an area inhabited by less than 10,000 people, you are also eligible for free management advice from the Rural Development Commission (see page 146). There are more than 30 offices across rural England and their trained advisors can tackle almost any problem. This is another first-rate source of assistance for the budding entrepreneur.

Small Firms Service
The Department of Employment (see page 149) runs this free, general enquiry and signposting service through various regional centres (refer to page 150). You can speak to an experienced counsellor either at your shop or in a counselling office. Three meetings are free of charge, with a modest fee being levied for subsequent meetings. Make the most of the service, as and when required.

Trade bodies
It is essential that you get in touch with your trade association, which can talk to you about:

- fixtures and fittings
- suppliers
- stock
- market research
- pricing
- advertising
- the law

and a host of other issues. Accurate and up to date information can be provided on request. Obtain the relevant name and adddress from *The Directory of British Associations* in your library. This is published by CBD Research Limited (page 145).

Solicitors
You must employ and constantly speak to a solicitor, especially in the formative days of your venture. He or she can:
- draw up a partnership agreement
- check a franchise agreement
- peruse freehold deeds or a lease
- handle planning applications
- draft contracts of employment
- advise on employment, health and safety and consumer protection laws.

The Law Society (page 146) can forward a list of solicitors in your area. Approach those who have been recommended by trusted associates. Pick one who appears genuinely interested in you and is on the ball with small business topics. Query high bills and change solicitors if you are dissatisfied with their services.

Using other individuals and organisations
Be ready to listen, assess and accept advice from any informed and unbiased source such as banks, building societies, books, business transfer agents, competitors, estate agents, insurance brokers, surveyors and so on. You can become an expert by taking advice here, guidance there and so forth. Names and addresses of organisations which are worth approaching are listed on pages 145 to 151.

CHECKLIST

1 Do you fully understand the workings of your favoured trade?

2 Are you aware of both the benefits and the drawbacks of being a self-employed shopkeeper?

3 Have you contemplated the attributes needed to be a winning retailer?

4 Do you possess all of these qualities, hopefully in abundance?

5 Have you decided whether to start a business from scratch, buy a going concern or take a franchise?

6 Do you recognise the pluses and minuses of trading as a sole proprietor, in a partnership or as a franchisee?

7 Are you familiar with the many and varied points which ought to be covered by a partnership agreement?

8 Have you consulted individuals and organisations which could assist you with your plans?

9 Are you ready to raise finance for your business?

2
Raising Finance

Once you have decided exactly what you wish to do, you need to start thinking about funding for your plans. You need to be able to:

- identify sources of finance
- recognise types of finance
- compose a business plan
- approach a lender.

IDENTIFYING SOURCES OF FINANCE

It is sensible to consider the different ways of financing either a start-up venture or a going concern, weighing up the benefits and drawbacks of each method before progressing.

Personal funds
You may be able to partly finance the business yourself, from life savings or redundancy money, by selling shares or cashing in an endowment policy. If a shop has living accommodation above it, you could put your house on the market, using any remaining equity for the launch of the firm. Clearly, self-financing avoids the cost of high interest charges on borrowed monies and the need to continually report and answer to a bank manager. However, you need to consider whether your funds might earn a better return by investing them elsewhere, perhaps in endowment schemes. Never forget that retailing is notoriously risky: at best, you'll make a little, at worst, you'll lose the lot.

Family and friends
Borrowing from relatives and/or associates can be a highly attractive proposition: a brief (or non-existent) examination of the viability of your proposal, easy terms and conditions, reduced or no interest to pay and often little fuss if you fall behind with repayments. Against this, you may be expected to be eternally grateful, to listen to a constant

stream of possibly half-baked advice and to allow them to help—more likely interfere—in the day-to-day running of the firm. With little knowledge of the practicalities of business life, they may suddenly want the money back, causing professional and personal problems for you. Such loans should be detailed in writing—amount, interest rate, repayment dates and so on—in an agreement that is drawn up by a solicitor.

Private investors
There are many individuals across the country who seek potentially profitable ventures in which to invest their surplus income and/or savings. Think carefully again about the pluses and minuses of entering into any form of partnership (see page 17) before going along this route. Then talk to your professional advisers (page 19), who should know of such people in your region. Commission a solicitor to compile a partnership agreement for you (see page 17). This will provide a safer and more solid framework to work within.

Banks and building societies
For most would-be shopkeepers, Barclays, Lloyds, Midland and NatWest are the main source of start-up and continuing financial assistance. They offer a wide range of services: loans, overdrafts, mortgages, insurance, life assurance, pensions, plus general information and advice on business and money management. On the debit side, interest rates are relatively high for small firms, typically at 4 to 8 per cent above base rates. Also, lending policies are much stricter than in the giveaway days of the late 1980s—a 50/50 split between your own and borrowed money plus over the top security for the bank's share is almost always needed in these difficult times. Building societies can be approached if you are planning to purchase freehold premises with living accommodation over the shop and wish to arrange a mortgage for the property. Once again, criteria are stricter and advances are less forthcoming than in previous years.

The Government
There are always innumerable schemes operating at regional and national levels which are created and designed to aid and sustain business start-ups including retail outlets. The Loan Guarantee Scheme is administered in association with the main clearing banks and other financial institutions. It is aimed at entrepreneurs with a viable proposition but who are unable to raise funds because of an inadequate track record or insufficient security. If the Government

and a bank believe the business will succeed, the Government secures 70 per cent of the borrowings with the bank allowing the remaining 30 per cent to be left unsecured. A premium of 2.5 per cent over and above the usual interest rate is chargeable with this scheme. Expensive though this may be, it could be your only option, so consider it carefully. Banks will provide more details (see page 147).

The Enterprise Allowance Scheme is operated in league with councils and gives an individual who was unemployed but stops drawing benefit, in order to start a venture, the sum of £40 per week for one year. To be eligible, you must have been unemployed for at least eight weeks, having £1000 to invest (which can be in the form of a bank manager's letter promising to lend you this sum), possess a sound idea for a decent business and be ready to cease claiming support from the State. There are no unreasonable strings attached to this money, so take it if you are able to. It is a useful sum, especially when you're setting up and trying to attract customers (refer to page 89).

Suppliers
Although not strictly a source of up-front finance except on rare occasions, suppliers of stock, equipment, machinery and vehicles can be of some financial assistance to you. Suppliers normally provide items on 30 days (or more) credit, subject to satisfactory references from your bank and trade associates, thus enabling you to fill and run your shop on their goodwill as long as you are able to sell goods quickly enough to pay bills when they fall due. Stocking a shop on credit can be done—and many retailers do it successfully—but it takes skill, especially during quiet trading times.

RECOGNISING TYPES OF FINANCE

Realistically, a bank will play a key role in the financing of your business, either now and/or later on when you may need assistance, perhaps to see you through a seasonal or lengthy slump. Be aware of loans, overdrafts and commercial mortgages, recognising which types are most suitable for your purposes. You also need to know about **fixed** and **variable interest rates**, plus **secured** and **unsecured borrowings**.

Loans
These are usually available for buying items of long term use. You may want one for acquiring and developing premises, or for purchasing a going concern and expanding it. Typically, they are set up with a repayment period of between two and 20 years, with five to ten years

being the average term. If you need a loan, don't plan to pay it all back in only a few years. You should not over-commit yourself to making large repayments in the early days of your venture, especially if you are starting from scratch, as you do not really know what will happen in the future. Ask for the lengthiest repayment period possible, making extra (bulk) repayments earlier if you can afford to do so.

Overdrafts

These are normally used for short term financing, arranged to ease a business through temporary cash shortages or for purchasing minor items of day-to-day use. An overdraft limit—perhaps of £5,000 to £10,000 for a small shop—may be agreed for a three- or six-month period with a review at that stage. Easy though it is to say, try to avoid muddling yourself into a position where you need overdraft facilities once you have been trading for some time, as they always seem to grow and grow until you find yourself in financial difficulties. Look on the need for any overdraft as an indication of weaknesses within your firm: perhaps debts are not being chased hard enough, payments are being made before they ought to to be and so on. Attempt to rectify shortcomings before the situation worsens.

Commercial mortgages

Increasingly hard to find, as financial institutions have been badly burned by the business failures and property slump of the 90s recession, these can be used to buy commercial properties, perhaps with built in living accommodation. Even if you come across a would-be lender—which is unlikely—stop before going any further and think of the huge financial commitment you would be taking on. You may feel that this added burden would be too much to bear in these uncertain times.

Fixed and variable interest rates

You will probably discover when borrowing money that you can negotiate either a fixed or a variable interest rate. The differences are self-evident: a fixed rate is agreed when the financial arrangements are made and applies throughout the term, whereas a variable rate fluctuates in line with changing base rates. Unfortunately, knowing which one to choose is less obvious. If base rates are currently low—perhaps 8 to 10 per cent—pick a fixed rate as they are more likely to rise than fall thereafter. Should bases rates be high—possibly 13 to 15 per cent—choose a variable rate as they will probably go down in the future. Between 10 and 13 per cent is no man's land and you must judge the prevailing mood for yourself.

Secured and unsecured borrowings

Security, usually in the form of a legal charge over a property such as
your house, is almost always required by a lender against any monies
borrowed, whether a loan, overdraft or commercial mortgage. If you
fall substantially behind with repayments and have little prospect of
catching up, your home can be sold to pay for your debts. Unsecured
borrowings—which are about as common as a dodo nowadays—do
not require security (although if you did not honour your financial
obligations the lender would still try to force you to sell any assets that
you possessed). If you cannot offer security, you may have to ask a
family member to provide it on your behalf or you could apply for a
loan under the **Loan Guarantee Scheme**, page 24.

COMPOSING A BUSINESS PLAN

A business plan is a document that sets out the proposed commercial
and financial activities of a prospective firm and verifies them with
detailed supporting material in appendices. This in-depth analysis of
all aspects of a (would be) concern serves several purposes. It can be
used to:

- raise finance, perhaps from banks;
- attract investment, possibly from likely partners;
- encourage assistance, such as from landlords and suppliers;
- improve performance, by enabling you to compare estimated
  and actual results.

Such a document normally comprises three parts:

- a commercial section
- a financial section
- appendices.

You can fill out a pre-printed form provided by one of the major
banks if you are seeking a loan, overdraft or commercial mortgage
from them. Alternatively, you may draw up a plan yourself, perhaps
loosely based around the banks' various formats. Although you do
not yet know enough about your imminent retailing activities to
complete a plan, it is worth thinking about it now. You may wish to
formulate thoughts and ideas for a provisional chat with a bank
manager, to gauge his or her attitude before returning with a

BUSINESS PLAN QUESTIONNAIRE

Every business plan should differ, depending upon what the reader (not the writer) wants to know. To start you thinking, list the key areas that are most likely to be of interest to the following people, and the reasons why. (Don't forget that a plan has several uses, not just to raise finance.)

	KEY AREA	REASONS
A close friend or relative	————	————
A prospective partner	————	————
A bank manager	————	————
A would be landlord	————	————
A possible supplier	————	————
You	————	————

Fig. 2. Business plan questionnaire

completed document to finalise borrowing requirements.

The commercial section

In this part of the business plan you must discuss the business itself. Outline its background: when, where and why it began trading, how it has progressed, its major achievements, obstacles overcome, why it is for sale and its asking price. Should you be planning to start from scratch, explain what made you think of the idea, why it will be successful and how, where and when you will commence trading. Then detail its location, discussing the site and why it was selected. Cover the property too, stating whether you are renting or buying it, as well as mentioning its price, terms and conditions, size, shape, layout and any equipment, machinery and even vehicles that need to be purchased.

Moving on, look closely at the products and services that you will offer: what they are and how they will contribute to stock levels and turnover, how and where they are made and/or bought, buying and selling prices, sales methods and how you will promote them. Compare and contrast them with rival goods and services; their advantages, disadvantages and how any weaknesses in your range will be eliminated in the near future.

Then talk about you, your partners and employees, as relevant. Without being biased discuss your personality, skills, knowledge and experience chronologically outlining your education, qualifications, work experience and so on and weaving in your attributes as appropriate. Describe your colleagues along the same lines, showing how their good and bad features blend well with your own. Refer to any employees, outlining their past and present positions, plus anticipated roles in your venture.

Detail the market in which your shop will operate: its size, the numbers and types of customers, your expected share, internal and external influences and their possible and probable effects. Also, review your competitors: their backgrounds, activities, locations, premises, products, services, customers and market shares. Set down all of their positive and negative features in relation to your own. Try to be wholly realistic, at the same time explaining how you intend to maximise your pluses and their minuses whilst minimising their plus and your minuses.

List your objectives in starting or buying a shop. Divide them into short term goals for the first trading year, medium term targets for the second to fifth years and long term objectives for thereafter. Keep your feet on the ground when stating these. Raising sales by 10 per cent, increasing market share by 15 per cent and opening a second shop within these various time restraints are all realistic. Bragging that you will rival W. H. Smith, Boots or Mothercare in the next few years will produce only hollow laughter and blow your chances of additional funds.

The financial section

You ought to complete a **profit budget**, on a clear and easy to understand form provided by any high street bank, which outlines your **anticipated sales, overheads** and **profits** (or **losses**) over a specific period, usually one year. Explanatory notes could be detailed too. Typically, you would fill in a month by month budget for the first year with quarter by quarter summaries for the next two years, if relevant. A standard example of a profit budget form is shown in Figure 3.

Many small concerns collapse not because they are unprofitable but as a result of cashflow problems. For example, a business sells its goods but has to wait three months or so for payments. Meanwhile, overheads still need to be met. With expenditure always exceeding income, the cash dries up and the firm ceases to trade. Hence a cashflow forecast—illustrating how cash comes and goes over a certain time, normally one year—and back up notes must be sketched out as well. Once again, the main banks supply the necessary forms. An example of a cashflow forecasts is given in Figure 4.

Having put together profit budgets and cashflow forecasts, you then should be able to set out your financial requirements:

- the total money needed and when;
- the type and amount of finance required;
- your financial input;
- what the monies will be used for;
- how and when loan and/or overdraft and/or commercial mortgage repayments can be made;
- any security that is available to set against borrowings.

Refer to your financial forms again and again to calculate your precise needs.

The appendices

Here you must put in any items which support and verify your earlier commercial and financial statements. For the business, you might include:

- three years' annual accounts;

- up-to-date books showing its current position concerning stock, assets, monies owed and owing;
- the business transfer agent's details;
- an accountant's assessment;
- a map showing location and surrounding area;
- the estate agent's property details
- the freehold deeds/leasehold agreement;
- a solicitor's assessment;
- a surveyor's report;
- photographs of the premises;
- vehicle, equipment and machinery details.

For products and services you could incorporate:

- samples and/or illustrations of goods;
- suppliers' price lists;
- quotations of various costs;
- retail price guides;
- advertising and promotional literature;
- competing product data.

About you and your team you might put in:

- curricula vitae;
- copies of certificates and diplomas;
- a partnership agreement;
- a franchise agreement;
- a solicitor's assessment of these arrangements.

Concerning the market, back up items may comprise:

- customers' sales records;
- customers' orders;
- a map highlighting the locations of customers and rivals;
- trade association correspondence;
- photographs of competitors' premises;
- rivals' sales guides.

Regarding finance, you should enclose:

- profit and loss budgets;
- cash flow forecasts;
- trade association correspondence about likely sales, profits etc;
- quotes and estimates of overheads and other expenses;
- proof of capital and security available such as bank statements.

	MONTH		MONTH		MONTH	
	BUDGET	ACTUAL	BUDGET	ACTUAL	BUDGET	ACTUAL
SALES (a)						
Less: Direct Costs						
Cost of Materials						
Wages						
GROSS PROFIT (b)						
Gross Profit Margin (^{b}/a × 100%)						
Overheads						
Salaries						
Rent/Rates/Water						
Insurance						
Repairs/Renewals						
Heat/Light/Power						
Postages						
Printing/Stationery						
Transport						
Telephone						
Professional Fees						
Interest Charges						
Other						
TOTAL OVERHEADS (c)						
TRADING PROFIT (b) - (c)						
Less: Depreciation						
NET PROFIT BEFORE TAX						

Fig. 3. Example of a profit budget form

MONTH		MONTH		MONTH		TOTALS	
BUDGET	ACTUAL	BUDGET	ACTUAL	BUDGET	ACTUAL	BUDGET	ACTUAL

	MONTH		MONTH		MONTH	
RECEIPTS	BUDGET	ACTUAL	BUDGET	ACTUAL	BUDGET	ACTUAL
Cash Sales						
Cash from Debtors						
Capital Introduced						
TOTAL RECEIPTS						
PAYMENTS						
Payments to Creditors						
Salaries/Wages						
Rent/Rates/Water						
Insurance						
Repairs/Renewals						
Heat/Light/Power						
Postages						
Printing/Stationery						
Transport						
Telephone						
Professional Fees						
Capital Payments						
Interest Charges						
Other						
V.A.T. Payable (refund)						
TOTAL PAYMENTS (b)						
NET CASHFLOW (a-b)						
OPENING BANK BALANCE						
CLOSING BANK BALANCE						

Fig. 4. Example of a cash flow forecast form

MONTH		MONTH		MONTH		TOTALS	
BUDGET	ACTUAL	BUDGET	ACTUAL	BUDGET	ACTUAL	BUDGET	ACTUAL

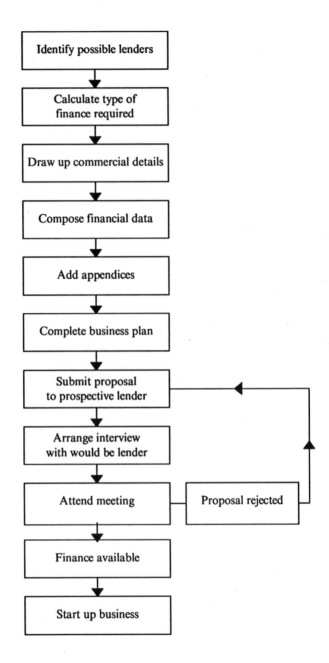

Fig. 5. How do you approach a lender?

APPROACHING A LENDER

Send an introductory letter and your business plan (or a brief summary of it if more appropriate) to a bank manager who has been recommended by local traders. Your letter might read:

'Dear Mr Mitchell,

I am a self-employed electrician who wishes to open an electrical appliances store at 4 Brandon Road, Felstone, Suffolk. I need financial assistance to start this new venture and have arranged to meet you on 4 September to see if you can help me. The enclosed business plan sets out my proposed commercial activities and financial requirements. It should supply you with all of the information needed for our meeting next week.

Yours sincerely

John Daniels.'

Arrive for your meeting on time. Adopt a professional appearance and manner. Be polite and courteous to him or her. Accept that he or she will spot and question you about glossed over topics, errors and apparent weaknesses and tackle any queries head on, working through them concisely and thoroughly. Always be scrupulously honest with your bank manager from the outset. Business is often conducted on trust and convincing him or her that you are a decent person will serve you well in the future, during prosperous and difficult days.

Hopefully, your (roughed out) proposal will generate a positive response, perhaps with an agreement to meet again when you have all of the facts needed to finalise funding. If your proposal is rejected, do not be too disheartened. See this as a learning process, find out the reason(s) and review your ideas. It may be that your approach was wrong with insufficient details being set out in the plan. It could be that the prospective venture is unviable. Listen to his or her opinions—only the foolhardy gambler presses on when everyone else urges caution. Such a person is destined for abject failure.

CHECKLIST

1 Have you considered who will fund or help to fund your venture?

2 Do you know which types of finance are best suited to your particular needs?

3 Have you sketched out a provisional business plan for initial discussion and subsequent completion?

4 Are you aware that this document has many uses, not least to allow you to monitor your performance on an ongoing basis?

5 Have you approached a lender in the proper manner and received a favourable response?

6 Are you ready to start up your firm?

3
Starting Up

You should now be ready to actively set about starting your shop. This involves some of the following:

- searching for the right opportunity
- taking vacant premises
- buying a going concern
- fitting the property
- stocking the shelves
- insuring your business
- opening the doors.

SEARCH FOR THE RIGHT OPPORTUNITY

If you are determined to run a particular type of shop, you must accept that you will probably face a lengthy search over a wide area before a suitable opportunity arises. The right shop premises or going concern will not become available overnight. It can take months, more likely years. Nor will your chance necessarily arise on your doorstep. You may have to move far away, to a new region. Be ready for a frustrating, sometimes heartbreaking search. It is far better to spend a year or so agonising now, though, rather than the rest of your life regretting a rushed, foolhardy decision.

Check *Dalton's Weekly* each and every week, either at the local library or from a newsagents. Shop properties and going concerns from Lands End to John O'Groats are advertised in it. Look through national, regional and local newspapers plus trade journals; even if you do not come across prospective opportunities, they will enable you to compare and contrast asking prices, sales figures, gross and net profits and so on. You could advertise for yourself, asking for landlords and shopkeepers to approach you.

Contact commercial estate agents and business transfer agents in your preferred areas. You'll find addresses and phone numbers in

LOCATION QUESTIONNAIRE

To set you thinking, decide where the following types of shop should be sited, and why.

	Where	Why?
● travel agency	———	———
● bakers	———	———
● booksellers	———	———
● greengrocers	———	———
● mens' fashions	———	———
● antique dealers	———	———
● hardware	———	———
● jewellers	———	———
● ladies' fashions	———	———
● fishmongers	———	———
● delicatessen	———	———
● camping goods	———	———
● pawnbrokers	———	———
● children's fashions	———	———
● off-licence	———	———
● sports goods	———	———
● health foods	———	———
● furniture	———	———
● confectioners	———	———
● toys	———	———
● butchers	———	———
● newsagents	———	———
● outsize fashion	———	———
● nursery goods	———	———
● jokes and novelties	———	———
● car accessories	———	———
● pets	———	———
● babywear	———	———
● carpets	———	———
● picture framing	———	———

Fig.6. Location questionnaire

Yellow Pages or from the National Association of Estate Agents and the Institute of Business Agents, page 147—ask for details of all empty units and businesses on their books. Dig deep for your golden opportunity; perhaps you're seeking a health food shop but an available delicatessen might also stock a range of foods which could be expanded and developed successfully, or you may have £20,000 to spend, but the £30,000 venture could have been overpriced and on the market for many months. The owner may negotiate, especially in recessionary times.

Drive or walk around cities, towns or villages where you would like to trade, looking to find To Let or For Sale boards above vacant units or shops. Get in touch with the relevant agent if any of them appeal to you. Keep your eyes open, and visit libraries and read newspapers to spot planning applications for or articles about retail developments or changes. Listen out too, you might overhear a conversation about a shop that is closing down or being sold. If you come across going concerns which seem attractive, contact the owners who may sell at the right price. Work hard—and on and on, without giving up—if you want to succeed in this trade.

LOOKING AT LOCATION

Location is a vital consideration when searching for premises. The position of your shop is a major factor in its success or failure. If it is poorly located your business will fail; you must make the right choice. You'll probably be planning to look for a prime site in a bustling high street in the busiest town or city centre. Forget it, this is unrealistic; these sites are owned by national companies seeking famous names as tenants, not you. Also, rents are so high that they'll cripple you financially before you've even started trading.

Most small shops are better suited to secondary positions in side streets, shopping arcades, on housing estates—even in the back of beyond. Everyday businesses—newsagents, general stores, bakers— may be sited near to a factory or school which should provide plenty of passing trade. Specialised concerns—high class confectioners, outsize fashions, camping goods—need not be centrally positioned either as customers will travel from far and wide for these products and services. In addition, the landlords of such properties are more likely to be individuals with whom you can establish a warm relationship. Rents will be lower as well.

Your overriding concern must be whether or not you will obtain sufficient customers at a particular site to sell enough stock to cover the rent, overheads and so on, whilst making a profit which will sustain and hopefully develop the business. See how many people pass by the premises each hour, day and week and talk to would-be customers. You will be able to make a more informed decision if you then take account of the neighbours, surroundings and nearby competitors.

Neighbours

Try to locate your shop near to others which attract people to the area. Supermarkets and DIY superstores—and their free car parks—draw in prospective customers for your business. Then look for complementary ventures to your own: ladies' fashion, babywear and wool shops go together well. A fashion store, fishmongers and undertakers do not. Many customers visit a parade because it meets all of their shopping needs in one trip.

Steer away from empty units, particularly those which look as though they'll never be taken, as they will have a detrimental effect on your trade. Not only do they appear unattractive, but they convey a strong impression of a locality which is going downhill fast. Some potential customers may assume that you're about to go under and won't want to buy your goods or services.

Newly opened businesses (like your own), especially in recently built precincts or courtyards, should be viewed with extreme caution. Face up to facts: most cease trading in the first year or so, leaving vacant premises that are hard to fill in a recession. Again, people will think your business is in dire straits as well. New precincts—on the edge of town, poorly publicised and slow to attract customers away from established areas—are a definite non-starter for you.

Surroundings

The general surroundings can help or hinder your trade. Compose a list of everything that may influence would-be customers in some way, dividing them into positive and negative features. Often, a plus for one concern is a minus for another. For example, a newly installed pelican crossing on a busy road between a supermarket and a parade of independent shops would encourage pedestrians to cross over to the smaller shops. However, an off-licence which derives much of its income from car drivers who want to pull over, pop in and drive off quickly would lose trade through the accompanying parking restrictions.

Consider these influences, and whether they would be good or bad for your business:

	Help?	Hindrance?

- playgroups
- schools
- colleges
- street markets
- farms
- banks
- traffic lights
- yellow lines
- parking meters
- one-way systems
- roundabouts
- car parks
- pedestrianisation
- bus stops
- taxi ranks
- telephone boxes
- post boxes
- newspaper sellers
- benches
- parks

You may be able to think of other factors relevant to your circumstances.

Always consider each aspect from every conceivable angle. Try to think of seemingly mundane and petty influences—for example, see where the sun shines. It's much more pleasant to walk on the sunny side of the street and the newsagent, greengrocer and baker located there will have more passers by, and gain additional trade, than those on the shady, cold side.

Competitors
It can be difficult to know whether to trade far away from or close to prospective rivals. The absence of any nearby competition may suggest this is the perfect opportunity—and you could be correct. Perhaps you are the only person to have spotted the need for a new venture. You may be lucky, a factory might have opened and you are in the right place at the right time to launch a business to serve its employees' day-to-day requirements.

However, no competition often means no demand. Try to discover if such a shop has ever existed in the area. If not, you would be unwise to press on unless there is a genuine and lasting reason why demand should have suddenly arisen. If so, attempt to find out by talking to the former owner, neighbours, landlord and so on why it relocated or closed down. You then have to decide for yourself whether these causes are relevant to your plans. He or she may have made mistakes—too large a unit, too many overheads, too much stock, too lavish a lifestyle—which you can avoid. External influences such as the decline of a major employer or industry, the growth of another shopping centre or town, might be insurmountable.

Of course it is more likely that you will face some competition, probably from small retailers like yourself. Visit them all over and again to assess their location, premises, marketing policies, staff and so on in immense detail. Spend as much time studying them as you do on your own thoughts, ideas and plans. Try to spot weaknesses which you can exploit: a small and cramped showroom, inadequate product range, ill-informed employees. No business is perfect in every way, make it your job to find and build upon others' faults.

Competing with big stores
You could be up against well known national and/or regional stores. Analyse them too, as fully as you can. Weigh up their advantages over you and your shop, such as an established reputation, apparently

unlimited financial resources, bulk buying power, a prime position, professionally designed and fitted premises, extensive advertising and promotional campaigns and credit facilities for their customers. The list seems almost endless. Dig out the disadvantages, though, and work on them:

- multiples' prices are usually fixed, you can negotiate with customers;
- their approach to customers is bland and distant, yours is friendlier and more personalised;
- their sales staff are hard to motivate, you are more committed and more knowledgeable.

TAKING VACANT PREMISES

As soon as you have spotted an empty unit in an ideal location, you must assess the property in more detail, valuing it and negotiating with the owner before pressing on to either buy or rent the premises. Never let your heart rule your head though, be ready to back off at any time if it is not the right opportunity for you.

Assessing the property

Visit the premises with the commercial estate agent handling the property. Make certain it is large enough to accommodate your counter, shelves, showroom stock, aisles, display areas, storeroom stock and so on. However, be wary of too much space; more sales will be needed to cover rent, heating, lighting costs and so forth, increasing your risks and chances of failure. If you're not sure how much room you will require, take a close look at other shops in your trade.

Think about the shape of the unit. A precise square or rectangle is often best, allowing you to set out your stock and other items as you wish to. Nooks, crannies, pillars, posts and alleyways are always a curse, stopping you from putting display goods where you want them. They also attract shoplifters, or thieves as they should be called, who can use them to hide or obscure their activities. Be cautious of taking old higgledy-piggledy shops; they arrange you rather than vice versa.

Decide what else you are seeking, depending on your own circumstances. You may wish to have a large window to display products, high ceilings to stack items up the walls, storage room to the rear, upstairs or downstairs, a backdoor and yard for deliveries and/ or living accommodation that is sufficient for you and your (growing) family. Contemplate the consequences of taking a unit that does not match your requirements. For example, a shortage of storage space

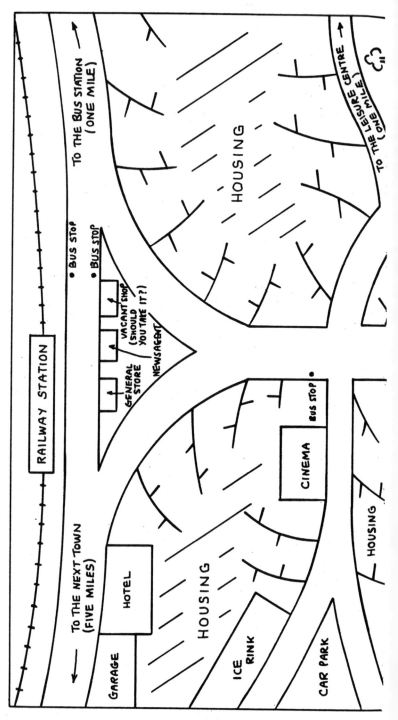

Fig. 7. Choosing

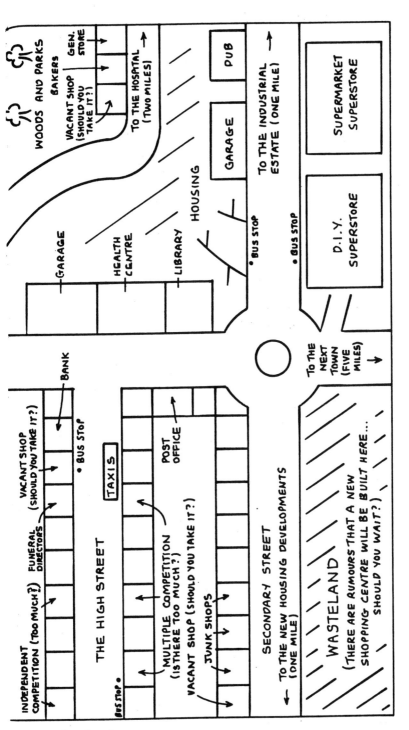

a shop location

may mean another property has to be rented at extra cost which will reduce your profits. This could make the difference between a viable and an unviable business.

Use this visit to confirm the key facts and figures about the premises: whether it is for sale or to rent, the asking price and so on. You must be sure that it is well within your price constraints and will not leave you short of funds in the early, critical days of the business. If the property seems to be structurally and financially acceptable— and make one or two more visits with experienced colleagues to convince yourself if necessary—then move on to arrange an independent valuation.

Valuing the property

Your proposed shop premises may be available on a freehold or leasehold basis. If it is advertised as a freehold property, it means that you are expected to buy it outright and become the owner, or 'freeholder'. Should it be promoted as a leasehold unit, it indicates that you may rent it as the tenant, or 'leaseholder'. You could take a new lease from the owner or buy an existing lease from the current tenant, or sublet it from him or her.

Freehold property

Faced with buying a freehold property, step back and think about the likely advantages and disadvantages to you. As the owner, you may have more freedom to do what you want, such as knocking down walls and changing your trade. If you sell your home and use the equity to fund the purchase you could avoid ongoing rental payments. Any capital gains from a subsequent sale would be yours (and the taxman's of course). On the minus side, if your venture failed you might be left with an unwanted, hard to sell property. Should you fall behind with a commercial mortgage, you could lose your premises, business and home.

Leasehold property

Similarly, you need to contemplate the pros and cons of being a tenant with a new lease. Typically, this situation arises when a property is newly built or old premises are converted into several units and the owner seeks occupants for five, ten, 15 or 20 year terms, as appropriate. In your favour as a tenant, new units tend to be standardised, easy to customise and need few structural repairs and little maintenance for the foreseeable future. Against you, these units are often left as shells with floors needing to be skimmed, walls

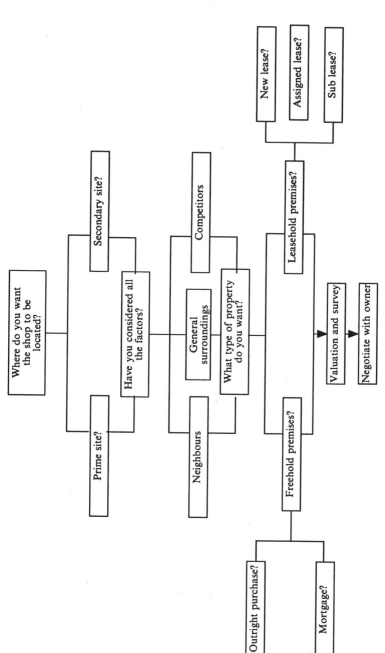

Fig. 8.How do you take vacant premises?

plastered and shop windows fitted, all at considerable cost. Also, new properties are unknown quantities, which may—or equally may not—draw in customers.

If the current tenant of the property wants to relocate his or her business or cease trading, he or she will try to sell, or 'assign', the lease during the term for an appropriate sum, or **premium**. As the incoming tenant, you will acquire a fully furnished property, hopefully in an established area. However, you will have to agree to the same terms and conditions as the outgoing tenant and you may find that the premium paid—running into many thousands of pounds—is extremely high and could cripple you financially.

An existing tenant sometimes wishes to sublet part or all of his or her leased premises if they are too large or he or she is unable to assign them. You may benefit from sharing a property, minimising excess space and splitting costs. Two complementary concerns under one roof can pull in customers for each other. Nevertheless, taking the whole unit as a sub-leaseholder is wholly inadvisable in most instances. The head leaseholder's inability to sell the lease is a bad sign, perhaps indicating that the property is poorly sited or has other unattractive features. The rent charged to you may be excessive so that he or she can skim a profit from it. Furthermore, he or she may want to re-occupy the premises later on, in better times.

Making the choice
Mulling over these thoughts so that you can put financial considerations into perspective, you then need to discover whether the asking price of a freehold property, or the premium and rent for a leasehold unit are fair. In the same way that you buy a car or house, you can only compare your prospective business premises with others on the market, by reading more newspapers and magazines and talking to other estate agents and retailers in the vicinity. Always employ a personally recommended surveyor, who should belong to The Royal Institution of Chartered Surveyors (page 148), to carry out a valuation and a full structural survey. He or she can further advise you on an appropriate price, bearing in mind any faults which have been uncovered by his or her investigations.

Negotiating with the owner
Having settled on the top price that you are prepared to pay for the freehold or premium and/or rent, you can make a written offer to the owner through his or her agent, setting out the reasons for the difference between the asking price and your offer, if relevant. You

should of course begin the bidding at a figure which is considerably less than you are ready to go to so that you have room to manouevre. A 25 per cent reduction might be fitting in many situations.

During the course of your negotiations, which may be especially protracted if other prospective buyers or tenants are involved (either in reality or the freeholder's imagination) you may need to convince a would-be landlord that your planned use is acceptable and will mix rather than clash with those of his or her other leaseholders. You might have to adjust your plans, perhaps selling childrenswear from 8-years upwards rather than 5-years to avoid competing with the nearby babywear store.

You will also have to show a future landlord that you will be a decent and trustworthy tenant who shall not be a nuisance and will pay the rent on time. Usually, references shall be sought from your bank and two trade suppliers, perhaps of stock or equipment. Alternatively, an accountant, solicitor or another person of professional standing might be acceptable. Even if you are new to business, you can still succeed: ask to meet the owner to show him or her your business plan, discuss your ideas and prove that you are a winner. Non-business references might then be accepted, such as from a residential landlord or even your old headmaster.

Most reference requests are fairly soft. A typical letter sent out by an agent on behalf of his or her client reads:

'Ms Amanda Stephens of 140 The Timberleys, Littlewick, Sussex, is proposing to lease business premises from our client at a commencing rental of £12,000 per annum. We understand this lady is known to you and would be grateful if you could confirm that she would prove to be a responsible and reliable tenant.'

If the estate agent is in charge of vetting tenants, with the landlord rubber-stamping his or her decisions (which is a common practice), you should find it easier to be accepted. Most agents just want their commission as quickly as possible, so the faster you're in, the better for them.

Once you have reached agreement with the owner of the premises— and do not exceed your upper limit—then the matter will move out of the agent's hands into those of your respective solicitors. A freehold sale will progress along similar lines to a house sale, with which you are probably familiar. The granting, assigning or sub-granting of a lease can be more complex as you will be signing a contract which is valid for perhaps 20 years. In either event, you need to employ a solicitor to guide and assist you.

Signing a lease

A lease is a detailed and legally binding document that needs to be perused by a solicitor who is fully experienced in this field, not necessarily the person who handled your divorce or Great Aunt Queenie's will. Every lease is different, with varied terms and conditions that you have to abide by. Make certain that you are happy with the terms in the draft contract sent by the owner's or tenant's solicitor, seeking if you can to remove or modify those that are onerous to you. Should the freeholder refuse, pull out and go elsewhere. Equally good properties are available if you look hard and long enough.

Most leases have certain common characteristics which you need to be aware of and ought to think about before starting discussions with your legal adviser. A lease often restricts the use of the property to a particular trade to protect other shops in neighbouring units owned by the landlord. Try to ensure that the phrasing is generalised rather than specialised—'clothes' rather than 'clothes for women, 35 plus'. Also make certain that the landlord's consent to change trades cannot be unreasonably withheld. If your business fails, you must be able to switch courses.

Liability for repairs

An '**internal repairing liability**' or a '**full repairing and insuring liability**' is normally incorporated in the document. The internal repairing liability makes you responsible for only the internal repairs and maintenance of the property. The full repairing and insuring liability means that you have to take care of all repairs and maintenance inside and out, and insure the premises too. Attempt to obtain the less extensive liability, especially if the building is old and/or in poor condition. Alternatively, ask your surveyor to draw up a **schedule of condition** on takeover, which sets out the precise conditions of the property at that time. You can use this to force the landlord to bring it up to scratch as your tenancy commences.

Rent reviews

Rent reviews are usually built into a lease every three to five years so that your rent is upgraded in line with the prevailing market conditions. At that stage, the landlord typically suggests an outrageously high rent which you have to haggle over. If you cannot agree, you may choose to sell or perhaps sublet to another tenant. Seek the lengthiest possible period between rent reviews; after three years, your business is only just beginning to become established and a rent increase or relocation to a cheaper site could be harmful to your trade.

When the lease runs out....
On **expiry of a lease**, the landlord is normally obliged to offer you another lease on the same basic terms and conditions as before, albeit with rent at the current rate. **Renewal** can normally be refused on these grounds:

- if you failed to maintain the property in a reasonable condition;
- if you persistently paid the rent late;
- if you broke any major terms and conditions of the lease;
- if the landlord wants to occupy the premises;
- if you occupy only part of the property and the landlord wishes to re-let it as a whole unit;
- if the landlord wants to demolish or reconstruct the premises;
- if the landlord can offer acceptable, alternative premises.

Other matters
Other **clauses**—and there will be an innumerable amount to be checked by your legal adviser—must be clear and concise. Too many leases are a jumbled, mish-mash of vague, legalised jargon. Try to have yours clarified where appropriate. Seek an arbitration clause too, so that in the event of an unresolved dispute you both agree to seek and abide by the decision of an independent person or professional body whom you mutually respect. Few leases have such a clause, but all of them should.

BUYING A GOING CONCERN

By the time you find a potentially suitable business with satisfactory turnover, profit, position, property and so on, you will probably have studied the details of countless going concerns and will feel sure that this is the one for you. Even if this is the perfect choice—and be ready to pull out at any stage if you have doubts—there is still some way to go before parting with your funds. You need to appraise, value and bargain prior to signing any contract to buy the firm.

How to appraise the business
Without announcing your presence, visit the shop over and over again at different times of the day, week and month. Decide for yourself if this is a successful and thriving concern that you wish to purchase and run. Consider whether sufficient numbers of customers are passing by, looking around and buying goods. Think about the ways in which the

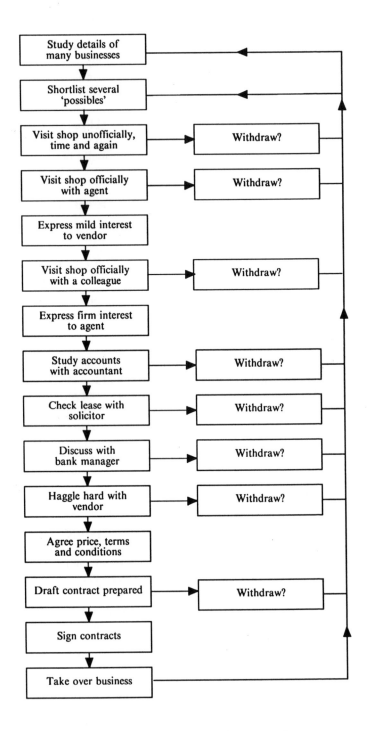

Fig. 9. How do you buy a going concern?

shop is set out and products are displayed. Draw in the atmosphere of the place, sensing if this is a winning, go ahead concern or not.

Making a formal visit
Then arrange a formal visit through the business transfer agent, or as appropriate. You want to talk to the shopkeeper about his or her business to discover its positive and negative features. You also need to confirm the exact asking price, turnover, overheads, profit, stock levels, equipment and freehold or leasehold details so that you and your advisers can accurately value the concern and your likely success or failure, taking into account your own circumstances.

Try to ascertain the reasons for the sale of the business. They will often be genuine: ill health, retirement, other commitments, even the understandable wish to sell a healthy venture for a substantial profit. Alternatively, these could hide the real, unpalatable truth: a new concern has never been viable, an established business is threatened by a planned shopping precinct, a local factory is closing down or an anticipated rent increase will slash profits.

Go into the shop with your eyes and ears open. See if it is different from your earlier, unscheduled visits. It may be cleaner and tidier. There could be more employees, perhaps they are the retailer's friends or relatives who have been drafted in to create the impression that the shop is busy and needs many assistants. Similarly, there might be an unusually high number of so called customers phoning in, milling about and placing orders. Boxes marked 'for collection' may be stacked in easy to see places. Don't be fooled by these feeble attempts to convey the appearance of success.

Also ignore all of the retailer's comments about 'immense potential'. If it's so great, he or she simply wouldn't be selling under any circumstances. Take no notice of the other 'interested parties' and 'imminent offers' that are mentioned at convenient moments; never be rushed or hassled into a swift decision. Other equally successful businesses can be purchased at a later date. Shrug off the inevitable compliments such as 'I can tell that you're made for this shop' or 'I'd really like to sell to you'. His or her opinions are biased and wholly irrelevant to you.

Take your time
Do not make an offer at this stage, however keen you may be. Not only do you want more detailed information to study but you also wish to negotiate as low a price as you possibly can. If the shopkeeper sees or even senses that you are enthusiastic, he or she is less likely to

negotiate over the asking price. Indicate no more than mild interest. Then back off, sleep on your thoughts and see if you feel as positive the next morning.

If you remain interested, pay an unscheduled visit a few days later. Again, see whether the shop has changed since that first, official meeting. It may now be quieter, with fewer 'sales assistants' and 'customers' on the premises. Take along a streetwise friend who just looks and listens as you chat through the main points once more. He or she may spot drawbacks which you missed. His or her presence could also worry the retailer who will be wondering whether your colleague is an accountant, bank manager or tax inspector keen to know about undeclared profits. See if he or she is as open and chatty as before. If not, ask yourself why this is.

Your next step
Next, contact the business transfer agent, expressing your firm and definite interest in the concern. To prove you are serious—at the right price—give the agent the names and addresses of your accountant, solicitor and bank manager, as relevant. Ask him or her to forward appropriate accounts and key documents such as a lease to them, for inspection and assessment purposes.

How to value the business
Assessing the value of any going concern is a difficult task. In theory, it is based on the difference between its assets (such as the premises, equipment and stock) and its liabilities (such as debts to landlords and suppliers of goods for business use or resale). **Goodwill**—linked to the idea that previous customers will automatically return—is also incorporated into calculations, at perhaps one-and-half to two times the annual net profit as recorded for the last trading year.

What the asking price means
The asking price is rarely if ever set out in terms of so much for this, so much for that. It will normally be phrased as, for example, £20,000 plus SAV. This means that you are expected to pay an all-in sum of £20,000 for the business with additional monies handed across for SAV, or stock at valuation. Usually, the vendor obtains outstanding sums and settles debts before the buyer assumes control. Otherwise, an appropriate adjustment is made to the final figure.

The past accounts
To decide what you are prepared to pay, you must scrutinise the

vendor's acounts with your accountant. Ideally, you should ask for—and receive if he or she has nothing to hide—at least three years' accounts so that you can see how the business is or is not progressing. If the concern is very new, and/or full and up-to-date accounts are not available, pull out now. You have too much at stake to take chances. If the vendor is genuine and the firm is as good as is claimed, then he or she should cooperate fully.

Fixed and current assets

With guidance from your experienced financial adviser, and with a useful back-up opinion from your bank manager, consider the lease, equipment, machinery and vehicles that are included in the sale, and whether you want to pay their assessed values as indicated in the latest accounts. Talk to estate agents and employ a surveyor to carry out a valuation and structural survey of the premises. Find out how well similar products on the market are selling, and at what prices. Take a close look at the equipment and other items, comparing them with secondhand goods advertised in *Exchange and Mart* and catalogues, and sold by shopfitters and at auction rooms. Also, decide if they are of use to you; they may not be if you are planning changes.

Study the **stock**, contemplating its content, level and proposed cost. Refuse to buy old, unseasonal and slow moving items that will tie up your cashflow. Do not purchase too much stock which will again leave you short of ready cash in the early months. Look at other shops to see what and how much they carry. Chat to fellow retailers and the trade association as well. Never give the vendor more than he or she paid for the stock. Don't be conned into paying current trade prices when some goods may have been bought months ago. Check the invoices very carefully indeed.

Consider the **monies and goods owed** to and by the business. You do not wish to take over with many (or even any) outstanding bills floating about, causing complications and confusion when you have enough other problems to worry about. Look for matters to be cleared up as far as is possible in advance of changeover, so that you can begin afresh with a relatively clean slate.

Goodwill

Pay extra special attention to goodwill, so closely related to recent profits that have been achieved. You and your advisers need to decide whether the stated profits are accurate. They may have been falsified for you; after all, anything can be put down on a single sheet of paper. Therefore, you must demand to look at the vendor's books and records (see page 75) for the preceding period(s) to check whether everything tallies and adds up correctly. Ask to see tax assessments and VAT returns as well (refer to pages 82 and 85) to find out what figures have been given to the Inland Revenue and Customs and Excise.

Bargaining with the vendor

As soon as you have established the maximum price that you are prepared to go to, you can begin negotiating with the vendor or his or her agent. Start by haggling over the assorted elements that comprise the overall asking price: the lease is grossly overpriced; equipment and machinery are old, out of date and of no use to you; only half of the stock is needed and the goodwill is not worth twice the annual profit. Be a miserable scrooge whilst bargaining with the opposition.

It is important to bear in mind that ultimately the sale price of a business is related to **supply and demand**. The vendor can say that he or she believes this or that sum is a fair price, or even that he or she will only accept a particular amount, but this is meaningless if no one is willing to pay it. You know that the vendor wants or has to sell and may be desperate to do so in a poor economic climate. If you sense this is the case, drive home your advantage as far as possible.

Even if demand for the particular concern is significant, always be prepared to withdraw from a proposed purchase rather than exceeding your top figure. Don't allow yourself to be persuaded into a heat of the moment deal which is against your better judgement and contrary to your long term interests. Business is financially risky at the best of times without starting with a shortage of funds because of a rash and foolhardy decision. Keep your money in your pocket and look elsewhere if you have to.

Signing the contract

Once a figure has been agreed, the proposed sale will be turned over to:

- the vendor's solicitor
- your solicitor
- and, of considerable significance if you are taking over a lease, the solicitor of the landlord of the shop unit, if appropriate.

Don't forget that he or she will wish to be certain that you will be a responsible and reliable tenant (see page 51). The solicitor acting on behalf of the vendor will draw up a **draft contract** which will be forwarded to your solicitor for your suggested amendments and/or approval.

Obviously your experienced legal adviser must guide you carefully through the contract, which is a minefield for the inexperienced, amateur know-all. Nevertheless, do read it yourself as well. Look out for, and if necessary demand to insert, several important clauses that will help to protect you. You need to ensure that the vendor agrees to keep the business going to the best of his or her abilities up to the changeover, running it as though not selling up. Also, try to work in the shop for a month or so in order to maintain a close watch on him or her whilst learning the tricks of the trade.

Making conditions
The agreement must stipulate that the vendor will not open a similar business within a given distance and time. You do not want him or her to launch a rival concern across the road from you, two months after the sale has been completed. A court will enforce such a clause if the stated distance and time are reasonable. As examples, if you purchased a specialised maternity clothes store, it might be fair to restrict the vendor to not opening a competing shop in 'the town' but unfair to state '50 miles'. When buying a newsagents, a reasonable distance could be defined as 'one mile' whereas 'the town' would be unreasonable. Limiting him or her to not opening a rival business for 'two years' is fair, 'never' is unfair.

Incorporate the condition that the vendor will indemnify you against his or her debts, just in case lots of unpaid bills start to surface after you have taken charge.

Other clauses, and there will be many, need to be fully understood by you so seek clarification from your solicitor. Never hand over any money until you are certain that this is a good contract and a quality purchase for you. Seek changes and amendments every step of the way, until you are wholly satisfied.

FITTING THE PROPERTY

You next need to prepare the premises, both inside and out, in readiness for the opening day. At the same time be thinking about how they will be maintained on an ongoing basis.

Outside your shop
Your prospective customers' first impressions of your business are usually based on your shop exterior. If they see flaking paint and rotting frames their initial opinions will be negative and valuable custom could be lost forever. Make sure that your shopfront is attractive and appealing before you open your doors to the public.

Even a lick of fresh paint can work wonders with a run down exterior. Keep it clean and in good condition thereafter. Also ensure that the forecourt and/or pavement are free of rubbish and mess.

The fascia

Your fascia or 'name plate' ought to be large enough to be eye-catching and sufficiently simple to read. Don't try to be too clever or obscure as any arty ideas will baffle most customers. A handpainted board, obtainable from a commercial artist listed in *Yellow Pages*, is striking and imaginative but may not be tough and durable in wintry weather. Perspex signs are longer lasting but can look cheap and tacky. Illuminated signs are increasingly popular, but the planning permission required from the local council can be a nightmare of red tape and pig-headed bureaucracy.

Instead of a fascia, consider purchasing a blind with your business name printed or painted onto it. 'Wet look' blinds—toughened plastic over metal frames—appear stylish and wear well too, if they are cleaned regularly and placed out of reach of vandals. Contact suppliers by approaching fellow retailers who have these blinds and seeking recommendations. After obtaining at least three quotations ask your chosen supplier to handle your planning application for you, as part of the sale.

The shop window

The shop window should preferably be large, wide and deep so that customers can see inside the premises. It must be spotlessly clean at all times. Wash outside and in at least once a week and more often if necessary (especially if you are plagued by sticky-fingered children). Any posters or leaflets which are attached to the window—and steer clear of controversial, customer alienating topics—should be smart and up to date. A peeling, fading poster advertising a two-month old event reflects a similarly shabby impression of your concern.

Your **window display** ought to be bright and lively. Have a topical theme such as Valentine's Day, Easter, Back to School, Christmas, with a central focus and co-ordinating blends of products and colours. Keep it clear and clutter-free as too many goods and ideas may be confusing and can detract from your basic message. At the outset, look for another trader's window which you admire and try to use their dresser for your own. Alternatively, enrol on an evening or summer school course at a nearby college. Always remember to change a window display regularly, ideally every week, to re-attract customers.

An open invitation
Once you have opened your doors in the morning, leave them ajar, day in and day out. An open doorway is inviting, almost drawing customers into your shop. A closed door is a physical barrier to mums with buggies and elderly people with walking sticks. It is a psychological one too, as many customers are reluctant to enter an unseen environment from which it may be difficult to escape from a determined sales assistant.

Inside your shop
Retain the original, solid ceiling instead of installing a false, suspended one as many new retailers do. You can then use it to display hanging goods (making certain that they are firmly attached to it). Paint rather than paper walls as this is cheaper, longer lasting and looks fresher. Choose a soft and soothing colour such as cream, grey or peach. Avoid cold whites, even those with 'hints' or colours which just make the walls appear dirty. Steer away from brash, headache-creating reds, greens and other violent hues. Walls should be in the background, not the foreground.

Lighting
Ensure the shop is well lit, perhaps employing a local electrician to fit strip lights along the middle of aisles. Pick 'warm white' ones which emit soft rather than harsh rays. Place spotlights in the window and at strategic points around the premises to highlight display areas. You may wish to install a timing device so that these light up for display and security reasons at night. Consider buying ventilation and heating equipment to keep the shop cool in summer and warm in winter. Check your powerpoints, to see that there are enough for your needs.

Floor covering
Do not cover your shop with a roll of carpet. Customers walk over it with wet and dirty shoes, cigarettes and food are dropped and toddlers leak everywhere. Filthy and threadbare, especially near the door and counter, you will soon have to replace all of it at considerable cost. Mezzanine tiles reminiscent of toughened ceramic are a foolishly popular alternative. They are cold, need to be continually buffed and cleaned to retain their appearance and are a safety hazard for customers who slip, fall—and sue.

Lay down carpet tiles instead, colour coordinating them with the walls. These are relatively inexpensive and damaged or dirty ones can be moved around out of sight or individually replaced. Contact nearby carpet stores—fellow traders may offer a discount—to seek their advice, look at samples and obtain quotes. Also telephone the cheap and cheerful discount advertisers in *Exchange and Mart*, who often sell direct from a warehouse undercutting retail outlets. The National Association of Shopfitters and the Shop and Display Equipment Association are worth calling too (see page 148).

Layout and display

You ought to display as full a range of your goods as possible, as many customers will not buy from a catalogue, and set them out so that all of them can be seen, thus increasing your chances of sales. Start by locating a special offer by the front door, attracting customers' interests and putting them in a buying mood as they enter the shop. Change this offer regularly to rekindle their interest every time they walk by or come in.

Once inside, they have to be guided alongside all of your stock before they reach the counter, by which time one purchase will hopefully have become two or more. Make this an easy journey to enhance their positive mood. Don't place large or heavy goods by the door as these soon fill arms, baskets and trolleys, and other potential buys will be left until tomorrow when the customers may shop elsewhere. Avoid putting soft or easily damaged items at the beginning of the route as heavier goods that are subsequently spotted will stay on the shelves. Aisles should be wide so that friends, mums with buggies and disabled people can move around in comfort. Be sure that goods on shelves are within reach of everyone.

Then encourage customers to spend their money. Spread special offers around the premises instead of grouping them together, so that people are tempted over and again rather than once only. Locate related goods close to each other to remind customers of associated items which need to be purchased. As people tend to look at eye level, stack the same type of goods vertically rather than horizontally so that customers are forced to scan up and down to compare prices and can see similar items alongside the ones in which they are primarily interested.

Site your **counter** at the end of your see-all route. Don't be tempted to place it by the door for security reasons, as many retailers do. It can damage trade: some customers will be reluctant to enter, feeling intimidated by your immediate presence. Others will come in but will feel ill at ease and are likely to leave as quickly as possible. Even if you don't trust customers—which is a very sensible attitude to adopt—

you must not make this obvious to them, otherwise they will never buy from you again.

How should you secure your premises?

Externally
You must defend yourself as far as you can against burglaries.

- Consider installing an alarm system, or at least a dummy box.

- Make sure that doors have solid mortice locks and windows have bolts, bars and/or shutters, as appropriate.

- Check that everything is locked and secure when you go home after work.

- Leave spotlights on overnight, especially near to the till.

- Never keep substantial cash sums or valuables in the shop, although a few pounds left in an open till may be enough to satisfy an opportunist thief and persuade him or her not to vandalise your premises out of spite.

These simple, commonsense precautions should protect you from spur of the moment break-ins, although the determined professional thief is unlikely to be deterred by them.

Internally
You need to take steps to prevent shoplifting by your customers.

- Arrange your layout and display areas in a sensible manner.

- Make certain that you can see all of the shop from the counter; neither pillars nor display stands should be allowed to obscure your view.

- Mirrors can help you and dummy cameras are an inexpensive, visual deterrent too.

- Be vigilant and on your guard at all times. Do not leave the sales floor unattended even for a moment.

- Have only one door open, to save you watching two or more.

- Ask customers to place shopping bags in a separate area.

- Chain expensive goods together and write brief descriptions on all price labels so they cannot be switched.

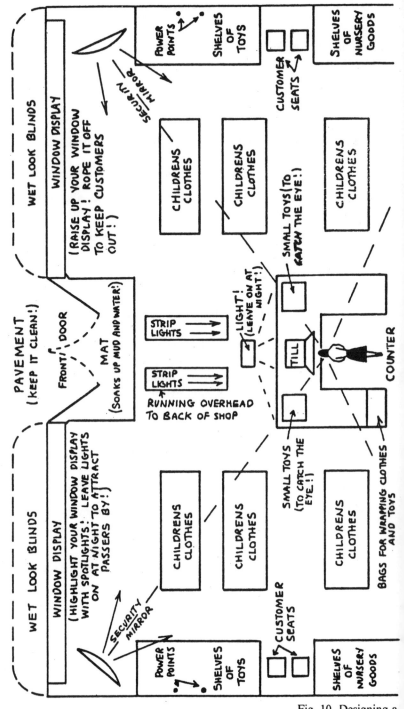

Fig. 10. Designing a

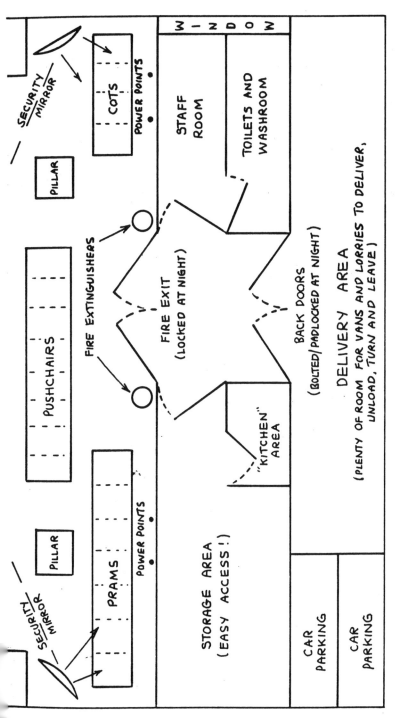

hop layout

Be careful if you think you have spotted a shoplifter. Do not approach him or her unless you are absolutely certain that an item has been deliberately stolen. To wrongly accuse an innocent customer will be humiliating and costly for you. He or she, and his or her friends, will not return and may even tell the story to the local paper which may be keen to splash it across their pages. Even if the customer has slipped something into a pocket or bag, they may simply be forgetful or could have been planning to pay for it after looking around all of the premises (or so he or she will tell the police and the newspaper reporter).

If—and only if—you are totally certain that a theft has taken place, wait until the person has left your shop. Approach him or her, politely explaining the situation and asking him or her to return to your premises where you can then telephone the police. If you are nervous of tackling a shoplifter or he or she runs away, you may prefer to call the police immediately, making sure that you can describe and will recognise the thief again. The police could prosecute a persistent shoplifter, although many offenders are released with only a caution. You can prosecute a thief yourself, but the time and expense is rarely worthwhile, as he or she will almost inevitably escape with a small fine. Prevention is better than cure. The crime prevention officer at your nearest police station can offer further advice and information, without charge. Contact the Association for the Prevention of Theft in Shops as well (see page 147).

FIXTURES AND FITTINGS CHECKLIST
- external sign
- strip lights
- spotlights
- carpet tiles
- display stands
- dump bins
- shelves
- counter
- till
- burglar alarm
- mirrors
- dummy cameras

MISCELLANEOUS ITEMS CHECKLIST
- open/closed door sign
- vacuum cleaner

- floor sweeper
- dustpan and brush
- first aid kit
- fire extinguisher
- tool box
- pricing gun
- paper bags
- carrier bags
- sellotape
- string

STOCKING THE SHELVES

If you are starting a business from scratch, finding first class suppliers, quality stock and equipment can be a hazardous experience. Often, you simply do not know where to go or what to look for. Fellow shopkeepers who are not in direct competition with you may be helpful, as could trade associations and journals. Alternatively, *Yellow Pages* lists local manufacturers and wholesalers which may be prospective suppliers. Your library also carries innumerable directories—*Kelly's Business Directory*, *Key British Enterprises* and *Kompass* amongst them—detailing traders across the United Kingdom and from overseas as well.

If you bought a going concern, you should have few problems. By working alongside the vendor for as long as possible before takeover, you will have met sales agents, dealt with their companies and become familiar with fast and slow selling products, profitable and unprofitable lines. Hopefully, you will then be able to step smoothly into his or her shoes, knowing where and what to buy.

Nevertheless, whether you are going to run a new or established business, it is sensible to contemplate what you want from your suppliers and the stock that you wish to purchase. If you can pay in advance or provide bank and other references for credit (and then settle on time), you should be in the driving seat with most suppliers. Be fussy, pick and choose from those available.

Selecting suppliers
Try to deal only with manufacturers and wholesalers which have a good name within your particular trade and a sound reputation for treating their customers fairly, being honest with them and so on. Spending a few minutes listening to another retailer's scathing, off-the-record comments and/or reading between the lines of a sanitised trade journal should reveal which suppliers can and cannot be trusted.

Can you pay cash upfront? If so, look for manufacturers and wholesalers which offer a **cash on collection** or **cash on delivery** discount of perhaps 7½ per cent or so. Should you be planning to buy in bulk—possibly getting together with other retailers in your region—seek those suppliers which give you generous quantity discounts. These may operate on a sliding scale depending upon the number of items purchased: one to six boxes at £20 each, seven to 12 boxes at £19 each and so on. Alternatively, you could receive a 5 per cent discount for orders over £500, a 10 per cent discount for those above £1000 and so forth. Make the most of these discounts if you can. They enable you to increase profits, if you retain the monies, or to undercut your rivals if you pass them on to customers via lower prices.

Do you need **credit facilities** to manage your cashflow? If you can supply satisfactory references, you will normally be allowed to pay either 30 days later or at the end of the following month. Seek manufacturers or wholesalers that are agreeable to a later rather than an earlier date if you need extra time to juggle your finances. Early settlement discounts—such as 5 per cent within seven days, 2½ per cent within 30 days—could be on offer too. You must calculate for yourself the financial benefits and drawbacks of paying promptly or slowly, but don't pay late as you'll destroy your trading relationship.

Take account of suppliers' general services before choosing.

- You may want them to agree to supply only your shop with a particular range of goods.

- You need to be sure that they can deliver well packed and undamaged stock quickly and on time. You cannot afford to order months in advance or to have empty shelves.

- After sales service must be reliable, with faulty goods being accepted for return with minimal fuss.

- It is also worth asking suppliers to sell goods to you on a **sale or return** basis, whereby unsold items can be sent back and credited to your account. Only those with confidence in their products—and they are few and far between—will agree to this.

Picking stock

It is important to pick stock that your customers wish to buy, regardless of your own tastes. Talk to them to discover exactly what they want from you. Some well known brands are essential, even if profit margins are slim, as customers tend to gravitate towards these.

For example, a Silver Cross pram will always sell well because of its famous, well respected name. Lesser known products, possibly with larger profit margins, can then be merged in to ensure a balanced and assorted range. Whether famous or unknown, goods must be safe and reliable. You do not want your customers to be hurt and/or items to be returned. If this starts to happen, they will desert you in droves, with many of them heading for the nearest court.

Make sure that you have enough stock on display and in the storeroom to satisfy your customers when they wish to buy from you. Promising delivery during the next day or week is too late in most instances—customers will simply go elsewhere. It is very tempting to keep stock at the barest minimum to retain cash in hand, and try to buy and sell on a step-by-step basis. Unfortunately, this is unlikely to succeed. You have to speculate to accumulate.

Don't carry too *much* stock though; it would be naïve to purchase every product in all sizes and colours, packing your shop with stock from top to bottom. This will tie up your capital, leaving too little spare cash to keep the business ticking over and pay the bills. Also, some lines and varieties will be slow sellers and you will probably have to sell them below trade price to clear them.

Of course, the optimum stock level, always sought but rarely achieved, varies from one shop to another. It can only be reached through a blend of flair, experience and luck. Trial and error are the keys and mistakes are inevitably made early on through under- or over-stocking. Given time, though, you will be able to strike a careful balance and maintain a level that is right for your business.

INSURING YOUR BUSINESS?

Do make certain that your firm is fully insured. A modest annual premium is a relatively insignificant expense. A fire or burglary is not: uninsured, and your business could be seriously harmed, if not destroyed.

Buildings and contents

Insure both the building and its contents—stock, fixtures, fittings, equipment, machinery—against the risks of fires, floods, storms, explosions, accidental damage, malicious damage and theft. If relevant, check with the landlord to see whether buildings insurance is already included within the rent or (more likely) the service charge to be paid by you.

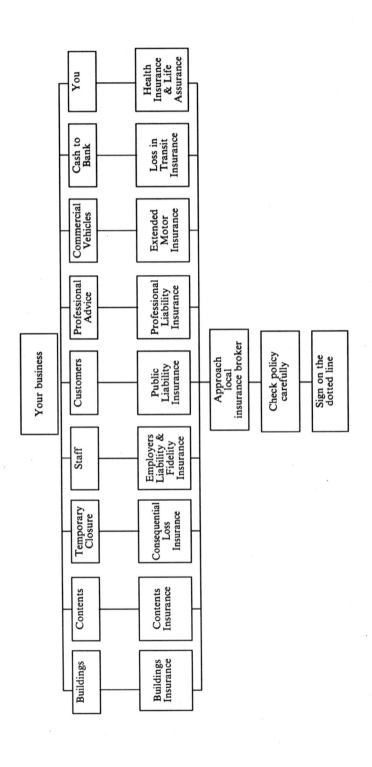

Fig 11. Have you thought about insurance?

Consequential loss

If your shop is forced to close down temporarily because of fire, flood and so on, you will need this insurance to recompense you for your loss of takings and any ongoing running expenses, such as wages. It may be included with the buildings and contents policy. If not, try to add to it or pay for an additional one covering this eventuality.

Employer's liability

Should you employ staff, you must insure yourself against claims made by employees who have sustained injuries or diseases arising from or during the course of their work for you. If a member of staff falls over on a slippery floor, traps a finger in a faulty till or is hurt by an incompetent colleague, you might be sued (see page 122).

Fidelity cover

Many workers (some jaundiced retailers would say most) steal goods from their employers, ranging from a handful of pens and pencils which are seen as a perk, to the wholesale ransacking of stock deliveries. Although careful recruitment and book-keeping are your best defences (refer to pages 97 and 75 respectively), this insurance is worth due consideration if you are concerned that excesses can, and therefore may, take place.

Public liability

It is vitally important that you possess this insurance in case you or your staff inflict injury or damage to customers or their belongings, or if they or other visitors are hurt whilst on your premises. Should they trip on a loose carpet tile or be knocked down by a collapsing display, they could make an expensive claim against you (see page 122).

Professional liability

If your work involves offering professional advice to individuals or organisations, you ought to protect yourself against the possibility that this could be inaccurate, or even harmful to your clients. This really is an essential insurance policy for all wise shopkeepers working in this field.

Commercial vehicles

A van used for delivering goods to your customers should naturally be insured with a third party, fire and theft, comprehensive policy. Do not forget to amend your private car insurance policy to cover business as well as social, domestic and pleasure usage if you drive it now and again for work purposes. Add relevant employees to any policies, in case they have to transport items on your behalf.

Loss in transit
You will probably pay your takings into your bank account in person, delivering them on a day-to-day basis, or as appropriate. Varying your habits, especially times and routes, will reduce the risk of robbery, and carrying small sums more frequently will minimise any losses, but think about purchasing this type of insurance policy if this is a concern to you.

Personal cover
Whilst contemplating insurance, don't forget to look at your own individual circumstances. Consider health insurance in case of accident or sickness which could cripple or ruin your business. Also check out a life assurance policy which will pay a substantial sum to your beneficiaries on your death. This is particularly essential if the business would collapse without you, leaving them without a regular income.

Choosing the policies
Approach a local insurance broker, who ought to belong to The British Insurance and Investment Brokers Association (refer to page 147), for in-depth information and guidance. He or she will visit your shop, recommend appropriate types of insurance and subsequently contact numerous insurance companies to find the most appropriate policies. His or her assistance is effectively free to you, as commission is taken from the company once a policy has commenced. (Don't bother to go direct to companies yourself, it's too time consuming, you probably won't find the best deal and the commission will not be saved, as the company retains it and charges you the full premium.)

Whatever your policy—and it is likely to be a comprehensive, combined one—always check it carefully, reading the small print and querying any pompous and jargonised terms and phrases. Ensure that it matches your requirements, perhaps adding a clause to take account of your large window and expensive blinds, or subtracting a clause and seeking a discount if parts are irrelevant in your situation. Do be sure that you obtain a 'new for old' policy whereby the price of equivalent new goods to replace damaged or stolen old items is paid in the event of a claim. Disclose all relevant information when signing forms so that subsequent claims are not invalidated.

OPENING THE DOORS

Before unleashing your hoped for torrent of customers into the shop, you need to:

- confirm that additional funds are forthcoming from your bank;
- open a separate bank account for easier book-keeping;
- notify the Inland Revenue that you are to commence trading;
- register with Customs and Excise for VAT purposes;
- tell the DSS that you are becoming a self-employed trader;
- inform the local council and water authority that you have taken possession of the property;
- ask the electricity board, gas board and British Telecom to arrange services from an appropriate date;
- contact Access, American Express and Visa so that credit and chargecards can be accepted by you;
- buy any miscellaneous items for the shop, referring to the checklist on page 66.

Then, learn all that you can about:

- doing the books;
- preparing and analysing accounts;
- handling VAT and National Insurance;
- conducting research;
- pricing products and services;
- promoting your shop;
- selling goods;
- hiring, managing, motivating and firing employees;
- employment, health and safety and consumer protection laws.

Do this prior to rather than after opening the doors. Work through mistakes in theory rather than in practice.

CHECKLIST

1 Are you prepared for a lengthy search over a wide area before you find a suitable opportunity?

2 Have you thought about the types of location that you should be seeking?

3 Do you know how to assess, value, negotiate and sign a lease for vacant premises?

4 Do you understand how to appraise, value, bargain for and sign a contract to buy a going concern?

5 Are you familiar with the best ways to fit out your property in an attractive manner, whilst securing it against shoplifters and burglars?

6 Do you know what you should look for when picking suppliers and stock?

7 Are you aware of the different types of insurance policy and which ones you need?

8 Do you know what else you should do before opening your doors to the public?

9 Are you ready to keep records for your shop?

4
Keeping Records

To retain control of your new and developing business, you need to be able to:

- do the books
- prepare accounts
- analyse accounts
- tackle tax
- handle VAT
- know about National Insurance

DOING THE BOOKS

Accurate and up-to-date books must be kept for several reasons. Regularly studied, they may enable you to spot potentially fatal problems in advance, such as high stock levels (which tie up working capital) and increasing sums of money due to you (which restrict cash flow). The Inland Revenue and Customs and Excise will wish to see accounts based on your records for Income Tax and Value Added Tax purposes (see pages 82 and 85 respectively). Your bank manager could want to look at your books too, if further funds are required at some stage.

The cash book
Divide a notebook into week-by-week pages and detail your daily takings, money banked, cash paid for stock and cash paid for expenses for each day. Draw up a weekly cash summary, perhaps transferring data across to a page at the rear of the book for easy comparison with other weeks.

The bank book
In another notebook, record monies in and monies out of your (separate) bank account, on a daily and weekly basis. Divide expenditure into individual columns for stock, rent, heat, light, power

and so on. Totting up these different columns at set intervals will show you what has been spent under the various headings. Always retain paying in books (not slips which can be mislaid), cheque stubs and bank statements for double checking later on.

The VAT book
Write out your day-to-day sales here, separating the VAT element in each instance, as and where appropriate (refer to page 85). Also jot down your stock purchases, overheads and expenses, with their relevant VAT sums as well. Sections can be added up in due course for internal assessment and submission of VAT returns to Customs and Excise (see page 85).

Creditors and debtors lists
Details of those individuals and companies to whom money is owed and who owe money to the business ought to be scrupulously maintained. For your creditors—to whom you owe money—record the dates of their invoices and when payments need to be made to obtain discounts and to avoid reminders, nasty letters and chasing phone calls. With debtors—who owe money to you—note when payments are due, statements and reminders should be issued and visits ought to be arranged. Tick creditors and debtors off the lists as debts are settled.

Orders, invoices and receipts files
Have separate files for orders placed by you and with you, invoices issued and received and receipts. For easy reference, place them in alphabetical and/or date order. This should make cross referencing and checking much simpler for you. Get yourself into the habit of keeping everything and anything. If your books are inspected by Inland Revenue and/or Customs and Excise staff, you will have to verify every penny of your incomings and outgoings. These files will assist you.

Assets lists
Equipment, machinery, vehicles and fixtures and fittings purchased should all be noted down, with their date of purchase, price paid and so forth. Permanent items of long term use to the business depreciate in value every year and an allowance—typically 25 per cent of the original value, then of last year's amended figure and so on—can be put in your annual accounts, reducing your profit and subsequent tax bill (refer to page 82).

The wages book

As a small concern, you'll probably employ part-time, Saturday and temporary staff to aid you as and when needed. Use a notebook to keep personnel records: names, gross wages, deductions, net wages, holidays and days off plus perhaps disciplinary and grievance records (see page 111).

General

Keep your notes comprehensive and updated, it's easy to fall behind. Set aside a few minutes each day to jot down takings, note cheques written, tick off debts and file orders. Check your books, lists and files every week, cross referring to the others to make sure everything tallies. Conduct a thorough review of facts and figures once a month, comparing your progress with your profit and budgets and cashflow forecasts. Prepare and analyse accounts on a quarterly basis to judge developments.

'Could you come back tomorrow when I've finished doing the books please?'

PREPARING ACCOUNTS

By maintaining clear and accurate books, you should be able to use the accumulated information as the basis of your (quarterly and) **annual accounts**. Although it is sensible to be broadly familiar with these statements, you ought to employ an accountant to draw them up for you from your records. He or she is fully conversant with accounting practices, tax rules and regulations and will prepare them to your best advantage. He or she will also give you a veneer of respectability with the Inland Revenue.

The trading account
This financial statement lists the **sales, cost of sales** and **gross profit** (or loss) of your business over a **trading period**.

- Sales are easy to calculate simply by referring to your books.
- Cost of sales is worked out by taking the stock held at the beginning of the year (**opening stock**), adding stock purchased through the year (**purchases**) and deducting stock left at the end of the year (**closing stock**).
- Sales less cost of sales leaves you with your gross profit (in this instance).

Sales		£58,000
Opening stock	£20,000	
Purchases	£25,000	
Closing stock	£15,000	
Cost of sales		£30,000
Gross profit		£28,000

Fig. 12. Trading account as at 30 September 1992

The profit and loss account
Compiled with and following on from the trading acount, your second statement shows the gross profit, overheads and net profit (or loss) of your concern over a given period. Gross profit is taken from the trading account. Overheads—rent, repairs, maintenance and so on—are then set out down the page and after being totalled up are deducted from the gross profit to give you your net profit (in this case). Clearly, your various expenses are easy to establish if full and complete records have been kept at all times.

The balance sheet
This last financial statement lists your firm's assets and liabilities at a specific date and indicates how its activities during a preceding period have been funded. **Fixed assets** are those permanent items such as

equipment, machinery and vehicles which are of ongoing use to the business. **Current assets** are continually changing items such as stock and cash that increase and decrease on a regular basis. **Current liabilities** are debts which need to be met in the near future, perhaps to banks and suppliers. Deducting current liabilities from current assets leaves **net current assets** (or net current liabilities). These are then added to or subtracted from fixed assets to reach **net assets** (in this instance).

Gross profit		£28,000
Overheads		
Rent, rates, water	£8,000	
Wages	£3,000	
Transport	£1,300	
Heat, light, power	£1,200	
Printing, stationery	£1,000	
Telephone	£800	
Depreciation	£600	
Professional fees	£600	
Postage	£500	
Insurance	£400	
Repairs, renewals	£200	
Miscellaneous	£100	
		£17,700
Net profit		£10,300

Fig. 13. Profit and loss account as at 30 September 1992

It is then necessary to highlight where the money has come from to run the concern over this time. The **financed by** section may typically be made up of sums which include your capital, any profit transferred across from the profit and loss account, loans from banks, building societies, relatives and so on. Your **personal drawings**—possibly for day-to-day living expenses—would be deducted from these monies to reach a final figure that ought to match the net assets (or net liabilities) which were detailed in a few lines above.

ANALYSING ACCOUNTS

You ought to be able to appraise your trading accounts (and those of any concern that you are thinking of purchasing) to see how well you have been doing. You can apply simple ratios to several areas which

Fixed Assets		£1,800
Current Assets		
Stock	£15,500	
Debtors	£4,000	
Cash in hand	£500	
	£19,500	
Current liabilities		
Creditors	£4,500	
Bank overdraft	£3,000	
	£7,500	
Net current assets		£12,000
Net assets		£13,800
Financed by		
Capital	£12,000	
Profit	£10,300	
Drawings	(£8,500)	
		£13,800

Fig. 14. Balance sheet as at 30 September 1992

will give you a rough and ready impression of your success (or failure).

Gross profit

Gross profit is often expressed as a percentage of sales which allows for an easy comparison alongside the average figure for the trade in which you work.

$$\frac{\text{Gross profit}}{\text{Sales}} \times 100 = x \text{ per cent}$$

Thus, for the trading accounts given:

$$\frac{28,000}{58,000} \times 100 = 48.28 \text{ per cent}$$

Expenditure

It can be helpful to take each area of expenditure, viewing it as a percentage of total sales. This is especially useful for comparing year on year changes.

$$\frac{\text{Expenditure}}{\text{Sales}} \times 100 = x \text{ per cent}$$

Therefore, for the rent, rates and water items listed in the profit and loss account:

$$\frac{8,000 \times 100}{58,000} = 13.79 \text{ per cent}$$

Working capital
It is vitally important that you know whether or not your business is solvent and can pay its way. You must find out how much working capital exists.

- Current assets – Current liabilities = Working capital

Referring to the balance sheet:

£19,500 – £7,500 = £12,000

Of course, if you had to settle all of your current liabilities tomorrow, it would be difficult to convert stock into cash very quickly, so exclude this from your calculations.

- Current assets – Stock – Current liabilities = Working capital

Again, looking at that balance sheet, the new figure is:

£19,500 – £15,000 – £7,500 = – £3,000.

Stock turnover
In any trade, stock should be kept as low as possible and turned over swiftly, freeing cash and making the best use of your funds. Obviously the rate of turnover varies, perhaps once a day for a bakery, three times a year for a clothes store, but it needs to be compared with trade averages.

- $\frac{\text{Opening stock} + \text{Closing stock}}{2} = \text{Average stock}$
- $\frac{\text{Cost of sales}}{\text{Average stock}} = x \text{ times per year}$

Hence, a check of the earlier accounts shows:

$$\frac{20{,}000 + 15{,}000}{2} = 17{,}500$$

$$\frac{30{,}000}{17{,}500} = 1.71 \text{ times per year}$$

Creditors and debtors
Be conscious of the speed with which bills are paid, both by and to you.

- $\dfrac{\text{Creditors}}{\text{Purchases}} \times 365 = x$ days

- $\dfrac{\text{Debtors}}{\text{Sales}} \times 365 = x$ days

Using the accounts once more:

$$\frac{4{,}500}{25{,}000} \times 365 = 66 \text{ days to pay}$$

$$\frac{4{,}000}{58{,}000} \times 365 = 25 \text{ days to be paid}$$

TACKLING TAX

Even though your accountant should deal with income tax and the Inland Revenue on your behalf, it is wise to have a basic grasp of tax matters so that you enjoy a better understanding of taxation when you discuss your specific situation with him or her.

Paying Income Tax
The tax year runs from 6 April to 5 April. Thus, the 1992/93 tax year spans 6 April 1992 to 5 April 1993. The income tax that you must pay for a tax year is based on the net profit shown in your profit and loss account for a given period (with a net loss set against other earned income for the year or carried forward or backwards to offset a future bill or to obtain a rebate). Once you have been trading for some time,

you will be taxed on what is commonly known as a '**preceding year**' basis. This simply means that your tax bill for a particular tax year is related to the net profit made in your accounting period that ended in the preceding tax year.

For example, Rajesh Munglani has a sports goods store and his accountant draws up annual accounts for him to 30 September every year. His tax bill for the 1992/93 tax year is linked to his net profit for the accounting year which ends in the (preceding) 1991/92 tax year, that is 1 October 1990 to 30 September 1991. In common with other self-employed persons such as you, various personal allowances are then deducted from the net profit leaving a residue which is taxed at the prevailing rates (20, 25 and 40 per cent in the 1992/93 tax year).

Tax returns are sent out in the spring, and tax assessments are compiled in the autumn of that tax year for settlement in two instalments in the following January and July. Hence, Rajesh receives a tax return in the spring of 1992. His accountant completes it as your adviser will do by writing 'see accompanying accounts' in the relevant sections and posting it back to the Inland Revenue with the trading accounts. The 1992/93 tax assessment based on the 1990/91 net profit is issued in the autumn of 1992 and is paid in January and July 1993.

Should relevant accounts not be submitted in time for the Inland Revenue to compose accurate assessments in the autumn, estimates are sent out (and tend to be overestimated to bring careless or obstructive parties into line as quickly as possible). If incorrect, you must appeal within 30 days of receipt, applying for a postponement of payment. Send your request by recorded delivery so that you know and can prove that it was received. You will need to explain why you believe the estimate is wrong, and the best way to do this is to submit accurate accounts promptly.

Opening and closing years
The 'preceding year' principal does not apply when a business starts and stops trading. For the first tax year, the assessment is based on net profit from the commencement of business to 5 April. If your accounting period runs to a later date (as it will inevitably do), an appropriate proportion is taken. For the second tax year, it is linked to the net profit of your first 12 trading months. For the third tax year, it is related to the net profit of the accounting period that ended in the preceding tax year or to the first twelve months trading again, if this does not apply. (However, if your second and/or third year net profits are lower than your first trading year's, you can ask for the assessments to be based on the actual net profits rather than those

for the first 12 months.)

As an example, Louise Davies opens her china goods shop on 6 June 1992 and her accountant compiles her accounts to 5 June annually. Her net profits to June 1993 are £12,000, to 5 June 1994 £18,000 and to 5 June 1995 £26,000. Therefore, Income Tax would be related to:

- 1992/93 (based on ten months to 5 April 1993) 10/12 × £12,000 = £10,000.
- 1993/94 (based on first 12 months' trading, 6 June 1992 – 5 June 1993) = £12,000.
- 1994/95 (on preceding year basis, 6 June 1992 – 5 June 1993) = £12,000.
- £1995/96 (on preceding year basis, 6 June 1993 – 5 June 1994) = £18,000
- 1996/97 (on preceding year basis, 6 June 1994 – 5 June 1995) = £26,000, and so on.

Had profits been £26,000 (1992/93), £18,000 (1993/94) and £12,000 (1994/95), Louise would ask for actual profits to be taken into account.

Similarly, the 'preceding year' rule is waived when a person or business ceases trading (which will hopefully be many years away for you if you approach retailing in a careful and thorough manner). The assessment for the tax year during which you close down is based on the actual profit for that period. If Louise shut her doors for the last time on 12 September 1998, the 1998/99 assessment would relate to the net profit from 6 April 1998 to 12 September 1998. The Inland Revenue may also reassess the previous two years' tax assessments, recalculating them in view of actual net profits.

Contact the Inland Revenue for background data on taxation and assistance with any specific queries that you have. Also request and read their informative publications:

- IR52: Your Tax Office
- IR57: Thinking of Working for Yourself?
- IR28: Starting a Business
- IR37: Appeals.

Check out page 148 for an address and telephone number to obtain more details.

HANDLING VAT

Value Added Tax of 17.5 per cent is charged on most goods and services in the United Kingdom, although some areas such as insurance are exempt and others including young children's clothes are zero rated. If your taxable turnover is expected to exceed £36,600 in a year, you must register for VAT purposes.

A VAT registered trader who buys products and services for resale and/or business use is normally charged Value Added Tax. This is known as his or her input tax. He or she adds VAT to the goods and services that are sold to customers. This is referred to as his or her **output tax**. At the end of each quarter, he or she tots up the output tax, deducts the **input tax** and sends a completed tax form and a cheque for the appropriate amount to Customs and Excise by the last day of the following month. **Surcharges**—starting from five and rising to 30 per cent of the tax due—are applied to habitually late returns.

Tony Reynolds, the proprietor of Tony's Togs, purchases products and services during a quarter which total £24,937 (comprising stock for resale and trading expenses). Checking his books, he calculates input tax at £2,876 (remembering that some items are exempt or zero rated). Total sales listed in his records for that quarter are £36,721, with output tax adding up to £4,241 (many goods in his range are zero rated). Thus, £2,876 is deducted from this sum, leaving £1,365 due to Customs and Excise. If inputs have exceeded outputs—as often happens when a concern is starting up or expanding—a refund would have been made to the trader.

For more details about the complexities of the VAT system—which you must understand inside out to avoid falling foul of the law— and to update these stated 1992/93 figures, get in touch with your nearest Customs and Excise office (address and phone number in the local telephone directory or see page 148). Ask them to send you two publications:

- Should I be Registered for VAT?
- Filling in Your VAT Return.

These tell you everything you need to know about Value Added Tax. Staff will answer any queries that you may have.

KNOWING ABOUT NATIONAL INSURANCE

You ought to be aware of National Insurance, which you may have to pay as a self-employed person (depending on your profits) and

Value Added Tax Return

For the period

For Official Use

HM Customs and Excise

Registration Number | Period

You could be liable to a financial penalty if your completed return and all the VAT payable are not received by the due date.

Due date:

For Official Use

Your VAT Office telephone number is 0752 600606

Before you fill in this form please read the notes on the back and the VAT Leaflet *"Filling in your VAT return"*. Complete all boxes clearly in ink, writing 'none' where necessary. Don't put a dash or leave any box blank. If there are no pence write "00" in the pence column. Do not enter more than one amount in any box.

For official use		£	p
	VAT due in this period on **sales** and other outputs **1**		
	VAT reclaimed in this period on **purchases** and other inputs **2**		
	Net VAT to be paid to Customs or reclaimed by you **(Difference between boxes 1 and 2) 3**		
	Total value of **sales** and all other outputs excluding any VAT. **Include your box 6 figure 4**		00
	Total value of **purchases** and all other inputs excluding any VAT. **Include your box 7 figure 5**		00
	Total value of all **sales** and related services to other **EC Member States 6**		00
	Total value of all **purchases** and related services from other **EC Member States 7**		00

Retail schemes. If you have used any of the schemes in the period covered by this return please enter the appropriate letter(s) in this box.

If you are enclosing a payment please tick this box.

DECLARATION by the signatory to be completed by or on behalf of the person named above.

I, ...declare that the
(Full name of signatory in BLOCK LETTERS)

information given above is true and complete.

Signature ....Date ....19...........

A false declaration can result in prosecution.

VAT 100   CD 2859-N9(02-91)   F 3790(JANUARY 1992)

Fig. 15. A VAT form.

86

perhaps as an employer too.

Class One
Of the four types of National Insurance contribution, Class One is paid by employers and those employees who earn more than £54.00 per week. Both employer and employees contribute on a sliding percentage scale according to the employees' earnings, commencing at 4.6 to 2.0 per cent respectively. The appropriate percentage is applied to the full wage, not just the amount exceeding £54.00. Under the PAYE system, the employer deducts employees' contributions from their wages and sends them along with his or her own to the Inland Revenue every month.

Class Two
This is payable by the self-employed whose annual net profits exceed £3,030. A flat rate, weekly payment of £5.25 is due, usually paid by stamp purchased from a post office and stuck to a contribution card, or via monthly direct debit which is more convenient. Should you believe that your net profits will be below £3,030 in the first year, apply for a certificate of exemption *before* you start trading as this certificate cannot be backdated nor contributions refunded.

Class Three
These are voluntary contributions at a flat rate of £5.15 for each week. Class Three is normally purchased by employees and self-employed persons who have not made sufficient Class One or Two payments to qualify for various state benefits, such as pensions.

Class Four
This is also paid by the self-employed, to ensure that they contribute as much to the State as employers and employees have to do. 6.3 per cent of annual net profits between £6,120 and £21,060 has to be handed over, with the precise sum being calculated and collected by the Inland Revenue at the same time as Income Tax.

For further information on National Insurance, and to update the quoted 1992/3 figures, contact your local DSS office, which can supply a range of useful leaflets and deal with individual queries (or refer to page 148). *NI41: National Insurance Guidance for the Self Employed, NI15: Employer's Guide to National Insurance Contributions* and *NI208: National Insurance Contribution Rates* are all worth reading.

CHECKLIST

1 Do you know which books to keep, and how and when to record information?

2 Are you familiar with trading accounts, profit and loss accounts and balance sheets?

3 Do you understand how to apply ratios to these accounts in order to appraise the success of your business?

4 Are you aware of the ways in which Income Tax is assessed and paid, particularly for opening and closing trading years?

5 Do you understand how the VAT system operates?

6 Do you know about the four classes of National Insurance contributions and recognise which ones you are liable to pay?

7 Are you ready to market your business?

5
Marketing Yourself

To maximise the potential of your retail unit, you must be wholly familiar with:

- conducting research
- pricing products and services
- promoting your shop
- selling goods.

CONDUCTING RESEARCH

It is imperative that you are ever alert to potential and actual market developments and changes, with particular regard to products, customers, competitors and your business.

Products

You need to know where your goods come from, how they are made, what their contents include, how popular and unpopular they are and what amendments and improvements are planned for the future by their manufacturers. Check your own records, read trade magazines, attend exhibitions and chat to agents and fellow shopkeepers. In many trades, manufacturers are held in contempt by retailers because of their arrogant attitude and poor service, and the grapevine is a good source of upcoming information, so long as you can distinguish between news and malicious gossip.

Customers

Be aware of your customers: who they are, what they like and dislike, where, when, how often and why they buy and what they want from you. Your customers are your business and if you do not satisfy them, you will soon cease trading and will deserve to fail. Talk to them at every opportunity, question them and act on their answers. If they want your shop opened earlier in the morning or later at night, then change your opening times if you want to succeed.

Competitors

Don't just study your rivals before you begin trading, do it afterwards as well, and on a regular basis. Keep comparing their plus and minus features with your own. Cancel out their advantages: if they offer a free delivery service, you should do the same. Take it one step further too—should they limit free deliveries to a ten-mile radius, make your area twice as wide. Promote those key strengths that they do not match, perhaps highlighting your 'price promise', whereby you'll refund or even better the difference between the price which you charge and that of other, competing stores. Visit all of the shops at least once a week, or ask friends to call in if you're now recognisable.

Your business

Always think through the likely effects that market trends may have upon your shop and try to act before rather than react after any developments or changes. If product prices are to increase significantly, perhaps attempt to stagger a series of short rises instead of one huge one. Should you hear that the nearby factory is adjusting its working day, alter your trading hours in anticipation. By doing this you will appear to be a market leader rather than a follower.

PRICING PRODUCTS

With a few exceptions, such as newspapers and magazines, you may set the selling prices of your products and services. Pricing goods can be a difficult task with many ifs and buts to consider. For example, low prices may increase sales but profit margins will usually be smaller, whereas higher prices could reduce sales but give larger margins. Prices that are too low or too high may both be disastrous for your firm. You need to strike a careful balance, contemplating several influential factors before reaching any definite decisions.

Talk to manufacturers, wholesalers and their agents. They will normally indicate a price (range) for their goods which you may or may not want to abide by. It is often sensible to fall into line with your suppliers' wishes. Those retailers who constantly undercut may upset fellow bigger spending stockists who might complain to the manufacturers. Those who overprice could anger their suppliers, who might believe that goods are slower to sell because of this pricing policy. In either event, supplies may become less readily available to you than to your competitors.

Check on your rivals' prices day-by-day, week-by-week or as necessary. For most customers, price is either a contributory or a decisive factor when choosing goods, so you need to know about your competitors', possibly changing pricing structures. Although your prices do not have to match every one of your rivals, they should be at least broadly similar across the range, and must certainly equal if not better those of well known products which customers can and will compare.

Think carefully about your customers and what they are prepared to pay for goods and services. Chat to them to find out how they define a 'low price', a 'competitive price' and a 'high price'. Everybody will give you different answers, depending on their viewpoints, but the overall response should confirm what would be generally acceptable and unacceptable so far as the majority of customers are concerned.

Your pricing policy could also depend upon the norm for your particular trade. Most have a broadly typical gross profit, perhaps 15 to 20 per cent for confectionery and 35 to 50 per cent for clothes. To drop below these parameters suggests that you would be unable to run a viable concern. To go above indicates that you might be uncompetitive in relation to fellow businesses. Your trade association or publications should advise you.

Most important of all, your prices must be linked to your individual aim: the sales you want to achieve, your overheads and the profits you wish to make. When you prepared your business plan you calculated the sales and gross profit required to cover your costs and leave you with the desired profit. If you keep a close watch on sales, gross profit, overheads and net profit as you compile records, you should be able to decide whether you need to adjust prices to achieve your targets.

Whatever you choose to do—and as with most aspects of retailing, trial and error is the required approach—always try to be flexible. Avoid having an identical mark-up on all goods, where you automatically add perhaps 50 per cent to the trade price of every item to determine its selling price. Use such a figure as a rough guide, not a binding rule. Well known comparable products may need to be less, unfamiliar and difficult to compare goods could be more. Drop prices on selected ranges at different times, such as 15 per cent off school uniforms prior to the new academic year. Overall, this will not significantly affect your gross profit but is an attractive sales ploy.

PROMOTING YOUR SHOP

You need to continually remind your potential and existing customers that you are still trading and offering a range of attractive, competitively priced goods as well as a first rate, personalised service, and you want to do this at minimal expense. A sustained campaign in the traditional advertising media—predominantly press and radio— is expensive. Imagine spending a modest sum of £500 and operating on a gross profit of 33 per cent. You must claw in an additional £1,500 over and above your normal takings just to cover that advertising expenditure. You are unlikely to achieve this, so look for other ways of promoting your business to the right people, time and again and at little or no cost.

Your window display

For a well located shop, a large window with an ever changing, eye catching display is its best advertisement. It will be seen daily by customers passing by on their way to work, the shopping precinct or home, and it should only cost you time, not money. Many successful retailers argue that their window display is all the advertising that they need to do—and in many instances, they are absolutely correct. (See page 60 for more details.)

Leaflets

A printing firm found through *Yellow Pages* or *Exchange and Mart* will advise you about and print leaflets for you, at perhaps a penny or two each. You know who you are trying to attract and can then go out in the street to find them. A car accessories retailer may tuck leaflets under the windscreen wipers of cars in local car parks. A nursery trader could hand them out to pregnant women—being careful not to approach overweight ladies by mistake—and mums with young children. Never put leaflets through letterboxes though, you just don't know who is on the other side of the door. Hand out leaflets every time you have something to announce, such as a new product range, or a summer sale.

Letters

Write to prospective customers to tell them about yourself and what you can offer. A personal message, brief, to the point and couched in a friendly style, should flatter and interest the recipient, encouraging him or her to at least pay a visit to your premises next time they are in town. If you keep careful records of all your customers—names (with the right initials and spelling), addesses (ditto) and purchases—you can contact them again and again when you have news that may be relevant to them. If they bought goods from you before, they may do so again.

Press releases
Often overlooked, these are certainly worth serious consideration. Local newspapers, and possibly radio stations too, are always on the lookout for topical news and human interest stories. If you have a potential feature for them, take an A4-sheet of paper and type or write 'Press Release' across the top. Tell your story over two or three double spaced paragraphs. Give your name, business address and telephone number at the bottom. Alternatively, phone them, cultivating a journalist's friendship for future use.

Word of mouth
Happy and satisfied customers impressed by your products and friendly service are walking, talking advertisements for your business. They chat to friends and colleagues who are seeking similar goods, and will hopefully recommend your shop. Even if you loath and detest the general public—in which case you're probably not suited to retailing—try to at least pretend to like your customers and to do everything you possibly can for them. That way, they will sing your praises much louder and more effectively than any press or radio advertisement.

There are many professional societies and associations which can help you to promote your shop more effectively, through various means. It is wise to check out their useful material and to seek their expert guidance and advice. The addresses and telephone numbers of these organisations, which include the Advertising Association and the Institute of Public Relations, are on page 148.

SELLING GOODS

If you are to run a successful business, you need to be able to sell your stock to customers face-to-face. There are no magic formulae for making a sale and no textbook can teach you when to smile or what to say when. Each salesperson, customer and situation is unique. Nevertheless, there are several dos and don'ts worth remembering.

Setting the tone

It is important that every customer feels welcome and at ease when he or she enters the shop. Having a large window, open doors, a distantly sited counter and so forth help to create a relaxed mood, and you can build on this by indicating that you are ready to assist if requested but will not approach unless asked to do so. A cheery smile or nod may be sufficient if a customer seems happy to browse. Should you be uncertain whether or not guidance is expected, a friendly 'Let me know if I can help you' could reveal the answer. If he or she needs assistance, then a 'May I be of help?' might be appropriate. In time, a sixth sense will enable you to tell what customers want from you, without asking.

When starting a conversation, perhaps in response to a customer's request for information about a particular product, you must be totally knowledgeable about your goods. For example, you should know where, how and when they were manufactured as well as your current stock position and how long deliveries take to arrive. If you can answer all of your customers' questions, they will believe that they are being handled by a professional. Feeling important and well informed, they are more likely to be in a buying mood.

During your conversation find out by asking gently probing questions and listening to what the customer says, exactly what his or her buying motive is. Perhaps he or she wants a sweater that is expensive with a designer logo to impress friends and colleagues. Alternatively, he or she may prefer a warm and cosy one, regardless of price or appearance, or a cheap sweater may be needed by the customer with a strict budget.

Knowing what is desired, you can stress the qualities closest to the customer's motive. Dealing with an egocentric customer, you might refer to a sweater's exclusivity and how it will be envied. If warmth is the overriding consideration, you could discuss the benefits of wool over acrylic, indicating the thickness of the material. With economy conscious customers, you might stress the marvellous bargain price.

Retain the customer's confidence—and win a sale—by conveying the (hopefully accurate) impression of a friendly and decent person. Strike a pleasant but not overfamiliar manner: attentive, respectful but ready to put across your balanced and impartial viewpoint. Neither argue nor constantly agree, which can be irritating. Don't just say 'yes' when the customer states 'That is the best one'; you'll be lost for words if they change their opinion. Take the conversation on a step further, perhaps with 'Mmm, what do you most like about it?' Give him or her a chance to talk, elaborating on the buying motives so that you can add relevant comments.

Try to be honest at all times. Avoid vague and misleading statements and promises that cannot be kept, such as about stock deliveries. Do not ridicule other products to promote the one that interests the customer—they may change their mind. Steer away from commenting either favourably or unfavourably on your rivals as this simply draws attention to their goods, rather than your own. Keep the customer's concentration on you and your products if you want him or her to purchase your stock.

Making the sale

Closing a conversation and making that sale can be difficult until your sixth sense has fully developed, and you know what to do and when to do it. Some customers make it clear that they want to buy the product, whilst others are indecisive. Don't let the moment pass, allowing the sale to drift away with the inevitable 'I'll think about it', 'I'll talk to my partner' or 'I'll come back tomorrow'—they rarely do. Politely and firmly nudge the customer in the right direction, perhaps with a 'Shall I wrap it up for you?' or 'Let me fetch a boxed one from the stockroom'.

Once the customer has decided to buy, you should take the goods with a smile and a polite 'thank you', wrapping and/or placing them in paper or a carrier bag. (Do not charge for your carrier bag, it makes you look mean and petty especially as they will be advertising your shop as they are carried). If the customer pays cash, check the amount of money given to you. Ring up the price of the goods on the till and count out any change before putting the cash into the till. This avoids any arguments about, for instance, whether you were given a £5 or £20 note.

Cheques and credit cards

Should payment be made by cheque, ensure it is addressed to you, has the correct date, that the amount in words and figures match and that the signature is identical to the one on the reverse of the cheque guarantee card. Making certain that this card has not expired, write its number on the back of the cheque yourself (do not let the customer do this as it can invalidate the cheque). Be very wary of accepting cheques from customers without a cheque guarantee card or for sums above the guaranteed limit. Some cheques will be honoured, others will not, and it is these which wipe out your profits. If credit or charge cards are offered—Access, Visa, American Express—follow the company's (variable) instructions to the letter, telephoning them in case of queries (refer to page 147).

CHECKLIST

1 Do you appreciate the importance of carrying out market research on an ongoing basis?

2 Have you thought carefully about the selling prices of your products and services, taking as many market factors as possible into consideration before reaching pricing decisions?

3 Are you aware of the best ways to promote your shop to the right people over and over again, at little or no expense?

4 Do you know how to handle customers on a face-to-face basis and persuade them to buy your goods and services?

5 Are you ready to employ staff for your business?

6
Employing Staff

At some stage, you will need to consider employing staff to help you with your workload in the shop. You should be familiar with the dos and don'ts of:

- hiring employees
- managing a workforce
- motivating a team
- firing employees.

HIRING EMPLOYEES

You must approach this task in a careful and analytical manner. Good employees who are friendly, knowledgeable, hardworking and so on are worth their weight in gold, and will assist you to build up your business. Bad employees who are late-for-work chatterboxes, keeping customers waiting, can destroy everything you have laboured to achieve.

What are your needs?
Start by thinking about whether you want **full time, part time** or **temporary** assistance. Calculate whether there is enough work to keep another person (or other people) fully occupied every day. Employing full timers is costly and time consuming: wages, fringe benefits, holiday pay, National Insurance contributions and the administration of PAYE, maternity and sickness pay should all be taken into account. Recruiting part timers (under 16 hours per week) and temporary staff as and when needed is far more sensible for most shopkeepers. It saves you an excessive wage bill and those other costs.

Then consider more carefully the exact work that you expect a new recruit to do for you, whether in the storeroom, on the shopfloor or on the road delivering goods to the customers. Compose a **job description**, detailing the **job title**, the job title of the employee's superior, the job

97

title of the employee's subordinates, the purpose and the main tasks of the job. An example of a job description for a sales assistant is shown in Figure 13.

JOB DESCRIPTION

Job title: Sales assistant

Responsible to: Shop proprietor

Responsible for: ....

Purpose:
- To assist the shop proprietor as required
- To sell goods to customers
- To take sales orders from customers
- To order stock from suppliers
- To check and store stock deliveries
- To handle telephone enquiries
- To keep the premises clean and tidy
- To run general errands, as requested

Fig. 16. Job description

Writing down your thoughts on a sheet of paper helps you to decide what skills, knowledge and experience are required to do the job well, and to prepare advertisements and application forms. It will also enable you to assess applications, appraise interviewees and judge the successful recruit at work in a more thorough and comprehensive manner. Always sketch out a job description and check it on a continuing basis.

Referring closely to the tasks listed in the job description, contemplate the skills and qualities which are needed to perform each one properly, building up a picture of the type of person you wish to employ. Compile an employee specification—also known as a job, person or personnel specification—setting out the precise attributes that you are looking for. You may wish to split them into essential and desirable requirements. An example of an employee specification for a sales assistant is shown in Figure 17.

Once again, the employee specification is useful on an on-going basis. Use it to decide where to advertise and what to put in advertisements. Compare applicants' details and candidates' comments about themselves alongside of it. Base interviews around it, noting down your views of each interviewee on the reverse side. Later on, the employee's performance can be assessed more effectively by perusing it.

```
┌─────────────────────────────────────────────────────────┐
│              EMPLOYEE SPECIFICATION                       │
│ Job title:         Sales Assistant                        │
│ The job holder must:  ● Have a clean and tidy appearance  │
│                       ● Be polite and clear speaking      │
│                       ● Have GCSEs (C+) in Mathematics    │
│                         and English Language              │
│                       ● Have sufficient strength to carry │
│                         heavy stock                       │
│            Should:    ● Have some previous experience of  │
│                         shop work                         │
│                       ● Be able to work occasionally at   │
│                         weekends                          │
└─────────────────────────────────────────────────────────┘
```

Fig. 17. An employee specification

Attracting applicants

Knowing who you want to recruit, now move on to decide where to advertise to reach the right type and number of potentially suitable applicants, hopefully at an acceptable price. Jobcentres are very popular with retailers, and deservedly so. Offering a free recruitment service, they can draft advertisements, advertise vacancies, issue and assess application forms and interview candidates for you. Similarly, advice and information on other key employment issues such as training and employment legislation is available without charge.

Schools, colleges and—often overlooked—careers centres are also worth approaching if you are seeking to employ a youngster, perhaps for temporary summer work. You can be assured of a steady demand for jobs at little or no cost to yourself. A notice in your shop window is simple, inexpensive and will be seen by many passers-by and customers, who might prove to be ideal employees. It can be a good idea to advertise in this way, although you must be prepared for some half-hearted and/or totally unsuitable people taking up your time at all hours of the day.

Generally, steer clear of employment agencies as well as press and radio advertising. Though they have many benefits, their main drawbacks are that they are expensive and unnecessary for the type of vacancy you are trying to fill. Also avoid word of mouth advertising amongst your friends and relatives. This may seem to be the easiest and quickest way of finding someone but it is unwise to mix business with pleasure. Close acquaintances may take advantage and you could feel awkward about disciplining or even firing them. Friendships might be ruined forever.

You need to design notices for boards at Jobcentres, schools, colleges and career centres as well as your window which will attract a small pool of high quality applicants from which to choose. Checking back to the job description and employee specification, give concise data about the business, the job title, location, purpose and tasks, the salary and fringe benefits, the type of person required and where, how and to whom to apply for the position. Such full information should enable readers to decide whether the company and job are suited to them and vice versa.

You might try something along these lines:

'Babytime requires Sales Assistant. A vacancy exists for an assistant to undertake a variety of duties in our small but busy shop. The successful applicant must be polite and well spoken and have GCSEs (C Grades or above) in Maths and English Language. Previous shop experience is desirable. We offer the successful applicant a salary of £5,000 per annum, 21 days annual holiday, a 5-day week with some overtime and a friendly work environment. For an application form, write to Jane Thompson at Babytime, 18 Generals Mews, Rustingleigh, Warwickshire IP10 8NG.'

Screening applicants

You probably do not wish to spend your time interviewing everyone who is interested in the job, preferring to use an initial method of assessment to shortlist perhaps six candidates who seem to be most suitable. You, or Job/career centre staff who are acting on your behalf, may screen by application form. With questions and answers laid out in a set format, you can swiftly check if essential and desirable requirements are met, easily comparing applicants. The form may also be used as a guide in any subsequent interview.

There are drawbacks though. If the type, number and order of questions are wrong, some applicants will not reply and those who do will be harder to assess. Base your application form, which can be drawn up with the help of the Jobcentre staff, around the employee specification, asking simple and straightforward questions which produce answers that enable you to decide whether your essentials and desirables are met. Keep the form short, asking enough questions to screen out unsuitable applicants but not so many that potentially suitable ones lose interest. Leave enough room for answers to be given. Ask for the details of two referees who can comment on the applicant's qualities. An example of an application form is shown in Fig. 19.

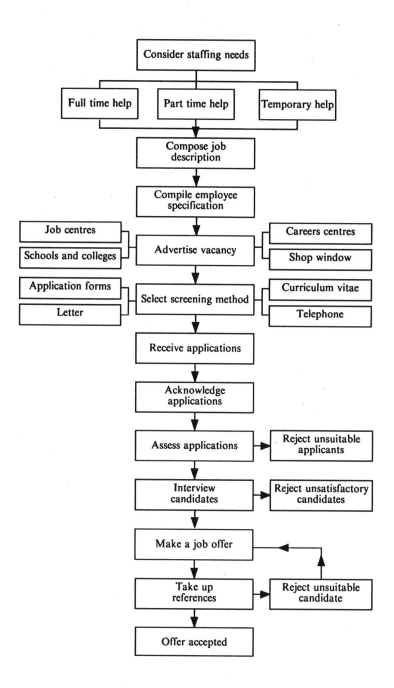

Fig. 18. How do you recruit staff?

APPLICATION FORM

Position ....

Name...

Address...

Telephone Number ....

Date of birth ....

Education

School/College	From	To	Qualifications

Employment

Employer	From	To	Job title and duties	Salary	Reasons for leaving

Hobbies

Additional Comments

Referees

Name	Name
Position	Position
Address	Address
Signature	**Date**

Fig. 19. An application form

Altenatively you could screen by letter, **curriculum vitae** or telephone. Letters allow you to assess applicants' writing style and may take up less of your time than drafting an application. However, some applicants may be poor writers but good at the job. For example, a salesperson is rarely employed for his or her literary skills. Curricula vitae—or CVs—can provide information in a logical sequence, making it easy to see if key requirements are fulfilled but allowing applicants to decide what to include. The telephone is a speedy assessment method, especially useful for judging speech and conversation skills. However, you are likely to receive lots of casual calls from half-interested applicants at all hours.

Acknowledge all applications, whether by application form, letter, CV or telephone, with a polite letter such as:

'Dear Mr Jones,
    Thank you for your application for the post of sales assistant. This is currently receiving our careful attention and we shall be contacting you again in the near future.

Yours sincerely,
Jane Thompson, Proprietor.'

This is simply good public relations for your business: applicants could be customers too.

Then compare the applications with the job description, employee specification and each other. Invite those applicants who appear ideal to come in for an interview. Send a letter similar to this:

'Dear Mrs Platek,
    I write to invite you to attend an interview for the post of sales assistant at 10.30am on 23 October at the above address. This interview should last for about 30 minutes and will be conducted by me. Please telephone if the time or day are inconvenient for you and we can make alternative arrangements. I look forward to meeting you next week.

Yours sincerely,
Jane Thompson, Proprietor.'

Reject the other applicants in a polite and courteous manner. Send a generalised letter to them along the lines of:

INTERVIEW QUESTIONS CHECKLIST

It is difficult to know which questions to ask at an interview. Here are some ideas.

EDUCATION/QUALIFICATIONS
- What do you most/least like about school?
- Why did you choose to go to that college?
- Why did you pick that particular course?
- To what would you attribute your success?

WORK EXPERIENCE
- Tell me about your current job.
- Which tasks do you find easy/difficult to do?
- What do you do in a typical day?
- What do you like/dislike about your job?
- Why do you want to leave?

OUTSIDE INTERESTS
- What do you do in your spare time?
- How do you relax?
- Tell me about your hobbies.
- Do you belong to any clubs or societies?
- What do you do there?

AMBITIONS
- Why do you want to work in this shop?
- What qualities will you bring to the job?
- Where do you want to be in three years?
- How would you describe yourself?
- How do you see your career progressing?

ANOMALIES
- Why did you not complete this section?
- Why did you attend four schools in five years?
- Why did you accept a drop in salary?

Fig. 20. Interview questions checklist

'Dear Mrs Kimble,
   Thank you for your application for the post of sales assistant. After careful consideration, we regret to inform you that you have not been successful on this occasion. However, we thank you for your interest in our hardware store and wish you well for the future.

Yours sincerely,
Jane Thompson, Proprietor.'

Interviewing candidates

Conduct interviews in a quiet room where you will not be disturbed by outside noise, the telephone or even the sun in your eyes, so that you can both concentrate on finding out if you are well suited to each other. Allow plenty of time to do this, with at least 30 minutes set aside for each candidate. Don't imagine as so many naïve retailers do that you can choose the right person by chatting over the shop counter for five minutes. You'll just be taking pot luck, and an unnecessary gamble with your own fortunes. Read through the job description, the employee specification and the appropriate application before every interview, preparing a list of topics and questions that you wish to cover. Typically, these would include your shop, the job and your plans plus his or her education and qualifications, work experience, outside interests and ambitions. Deal with anomalies too: gaps in the application form, brief explanations and so on.

   Greet each interviewee with a genuine smile, putting him or her at ease by chatting informally, possibly about your business, its goods and services and the job itself. As you're talking, guide the interviewee along to the interview room, consequently showing him or her to a seat. When he or she starts to converse freely, press ahead to discuss the various subjects, asking questions where relevant. Try not to talk too much though, but encourage the interviewee to speak by smiling and nodding, listening to what is said so that you can compare him or her with the employee specification and moving the conversation along with another questions when you've heard what you want to know. At the end, let him or her ask you questions and answer them as fully and as honestly as you can.

   Finish by standing up to signal the interview is over, thanking him or her for coming in and saying you will be in touch shortly. Show him or her to the door, bidding farewell in a warm and friendly manner. Don't make a decision on the spot however much you may admire an interviewee, as you really need time to think and to compare and contrast interviewees. After all of the interviews have been completed, study the job description, employee specification and the applications again, whilst contemplating how each interviewee fared in their interview. Decide who seems to be best suited to the job, keeping one or two others in reserve in case he or she turns down your offer.

Making a job offer

Put your job offer to your favoured candidate in writing, to avoid possible misunderstandings and confusion. You might write:

'Dear Mr Hicks,

Further to our meeting, I am pleased to offer you employment as a sales assistant at Babytime. Your hours of work will be 9am to 5pm from Monday to Friday, with one hour lunchbreaks to be taken at agreeable times. Your wage of £100 per week will be paid in cash every Friday afternoon. You will be entitled to 21 days' paid holiday per year plus statutory holidays. Other, previously discussed terms of employment will be detailed in writing once you have begun work. Please confirm if you wish to accept this offer and when you will be able to commence work. As the offer is subject to the receipt of satisfactory references, can you also confirm that I may now approach your referees.

Yours sincerely,
Jane Thompson, Proprietor'.

Once permission has been given, take up references to check facts and verify your opinions. These ought to be supplied by current and/or former employers plus schoolteachers or college lecturers for young people. Write to referees to introduce yourself and to ask them to talk to you on the telephone, as you will be able to question them more fully and obtain off the record, candid comments that might not be stated in writing. When discussing the chosen candidate, ask about his or her:

- length of employment
- job
- conduct
- time-keeping
- abilities

- honesty
- health
- reasons for leaving

Also raise the crunch question 'Would you re-employ him or her?' This can be revealing.

As soon as your offer is accepted and quality references have been provided (and turn to your second candidate if they are not) you must reject the remaining interviewees. As before, do this in a friendly manner, remembering that they may be customers too and could be ideal for other jobs in the future. They will not apply if you have offended them. Send a letter along the lines of the one which was distributed to rejected applicants, page 105. Do not specify a reason for rejection as this can lead to ill feeling and arguments as some unsuccessful candidates may try to convince you that you are wrong. If pressurised, indicate that it was a very close and tough decision to make but that the successful candidate had that little bit of extra experience, or whatever.

MANAGING A WORKFORCE

Handling employees can be a perpetual headache unless you know what you should be doing, especially with regard to the commencement of employment, pay and financial matters, holidays and time off plus rules and procedures.

Commencing employment

Settling into a new job is never easy. Do your best to help by inviting every recruit to spend some time with you in the shop before he or she starts work. Talk about your business once more: products and services, the marketplace, your plans and so on. Allow him or her to soak in the atmosphere, seeing around the premises, watching you take stock deliveries, deal with customers and tackle complaints. Chat about the work: hours, rules, procedures and so forth. Let him or her spend some time with new colleagues. See this as an opportunity to get to know each other and to establish a friendly, working relationship.

On the first day, be certain that you have set aside a coathook, a clean and tidy place for personal belongings and even a mug for tea or coffee, to make him or her feel welcome. Tell staff that your new employee is coming in, to ensure that they make them feel at ease. Meet the new worker personally to talk through the day's work and any worries that they have. Then if relevant pass him or her over to an

STATEMENT OF TERMS OF EMPLOYMENT

This statement sets out the terms of employment on which Jane Thompson (the employer) employs James Hicks (the employee) from 16 November 1992.

1. The employee is employed as a sales assistant.

2. The rate of pay is £100 per week, paid in cash every Friday afternoon.

3. The hours of work are from 9am to 5pm from Monday to Friday inclusive, with lunchbreaks between 12.30pm and 1.30pm.

4. The employee is entitled to 21 days' paid holiday each year, to be taken at mutually agreed times.

5. Disciplinary and grievance rules and procedures are detailed in the attached notes.

6. Statutory sick pay is paid in accordance with legal requirements. *Sick or Disabled* is attached for reference purposes.

7. The employer has made no provision for a pension scheme.

8. Notice must be given in line with statutory requirements. *Rights to Notice and Reasons for Dismissal* is attached for reference purposes.

Signature:.................... Date:......................

Signature:.................... Date:......................

Fig. 21. A Statement of the Terms of Employment

experienced assistant for guidance. Continually check on progress throughout the day, regularly asking if there are any queries or problems which you can try to resolve.

Monitor all new staff closely from the beginning to appraise developments, deal with worries and eliminate difficulties as far as possible. Any gaps that appear to exist in their knowledge or experience may need to be rectified by additional training, either by you or perhaps via a day release course at a local college. Assess progress to spot and develop strengths, recognise and remedy weaknesses, and identify and attend to prospective pitfalls at the earliest stage.

Within 13 weeks of starting work, those employees who work for 16 hours or so each week (or who have been employed for eight hours or more for five years) are legally entitled to receive a written statement of the main terms of employment from you. This information should be detailed within it, or in other accessible documents to which reference is made:

- the employer's and employee's names;
- the date when employment began;
- the job title;
- the hours of work;
- the rate and intervals of pay;
- holiday and sickness pay and arrangements;
- pension arrangements;
- disciplinary and grievance rules and procedures;
- notice arrangements.

An example of a written statement is on page 108. For further details, contact the Department of Employment (see page 149) and read their booklet *Written Statement of the Main Terms and Conditions of Employment*.

Pay and financial matters

It is difficult to know how much to pay your staff. Reach a decision by chatting to Jobcentre employees and fellow retailers about the going rates. £3.50 to £4 per hour for a sales assistant may be suitable in 1992. Try to match, if not slightly better, whatever else is on offer if you wish to attract and retain quality workers. You will probably be expected to pay employees in cash or by cheque on a weekly basis. When you do, be aware that those who work for 16 hours or so per week (or from eight to 16 hours each week for five years) are entitled to itemised pay statements from you. Such a statement should set out the gross wage, the amount and purpose of any deductions and the net wage. The Department of Employment publishes useful booklets on this subject: *The Law on the Payment of Wages and Deductions* and *Itemised Pay Statements*. Peruse them from cover to cover.

An an employer, you may have to administer the headache inducing **Pay As You Earn (PAYE)** scheme whereby Income Tax and National Insurance contributions have to be deducted from employees' wages and forwarded to the Inland Revenue each month. Operating instructions are provided by the local PAYE tax office on request. Also study their booklets *Employer's Guide to PAYE* and *Employer's Guide to National Insurance Contributions*. The DSS can supply a helpful booklet too: CF139, *National Insurance Tables*.

All of your employees who earn more than the lower earnings limit for National Insurance contributions (£54.00 in 1992/93, see page 87), might be entitled to **Statutory Sick Pay (SSP)** from you for up to 28 weeks of sickness. Those who earn between £54.00 and £189.95 each week may be eligible to receive £45.30 SSP each week. Employees earning £190.00 or more could be entitled to £52.50 (1992/93). You can reclaim SSP sums from the State by deducting the relevant amounts from National Insurance contributions paid through the PAYE system. SSP entitlements and arrangements are ludicrously complex and tangled matters, and you must read these DSS leaflets in some detail: NI 227, *Employer's Guide to Statutory Sick Pay*; NI 196, *Social Security Benefit Rates* and FB28, *Sick or Disabled*. Then take advice from your local DSS office.

The majority of employees who have been employed by you for six months, who have average weekly earnings equal to or above the National Insurance lower earnings limit and who stop work because of pregnancy are entitled to up to 18 weeks' **Statutory Maternity Pay (SMP)** from you. Employees who have worked for 16 hours or more each week for two years (or some eight to 16 hours per week for five years) may receive 90 per cent of their average weekly earnings for six weeks followed by a flat, statutory weekly rate of £46.30 (1992/93) for up to another 12 weeks. Those who have been employed for between six months and two years would be eligible to the flat rate for up to 18 weeks. As with SSP, Statutory Maternity Pay can be claimed back from the State via the PAYE system. Read the DSS leaflet NI 257, *Employer's Guide to Statutory Maternity Pay* and seek guidance from their nearest office.

Be conscious that most pregnant workers have other statutory rights as well. They may be entitled to reasonable paid time off to attend antenatal clinics (regardless of hours worked or length of service), to return to work after the birth of the baby (although employers with no more than five employees do not need to keep jobs available) and to claim unfair dismissal if sacked because of pregnancy. Maternity benefits are as complicated to understand as SSP is, with innumerable (major and minor) conditions being attached to each of them. Gain a fuller insight into this topic by studying these DSS leaflets: NI 17A, *A Guide to Maternity Benefits* and FB8, *Babies and Benefits*.

Holidays and time off
Employees will expect a reasonable, paid holiday entitlement according to their status. Begin by giving 18 days (plus public and bank holidays) to junior staff, subsequently increasing this to possibly 25 days (plus statutory holidays), depending upon their length of service. As well as giving reasonable paid time off to pregnant employees for antenatal care, it must also be offered to those employees under notice of redundancy who have worked for 16 hours or more for two years (or eight hours or so for five years) who wish to look for work or training opportunities (see page 117). Workers who perform public duties such as jury service are entitled to reasonable unpaid time off. Use your discretion when an employee suffers a bereavement, it would be hardhearted not to allow them to take (paid) time off.

Rules and procedures
As a responsible employer, you ought to set out disciplinary and grievance rules and procedures in writing, handing this information to employees with their written statements and displaying it in a staff area too. Rules help to establish the levels of performance and behaviour that are expected from workers. Procedures assist you to handle situations where rules have been breached and (hopefully) will ensure that they are not broken again. Make certain that your staff are fully aware of and conversant with all of your rules and procedures, explaining them one by one if necessary.

Disciplinary rules must vary from one employer to another, according to individual circumstances. It is up to you to decide upon and set your own ones. Ensure that your employees know what you consider to be unacceptable conduct. Such matters as unexcused lateness or absence, inappropriate appearance or dress and overlong lunchbreaks may be looked upon as minor misconduct, which might lead to disciplinary procedures being implemented if repeated. Continual, unauthorised lateness or absences, the inability to meet standards and doing other work during the hours of employment could be viewed as examples of serious misconduct that will initiate disciplinary action. Theft, abusive behaviour, assault, breaches of confidentiality and other extreme activities might be termed as gross misconduct which may warrant immediate dismissal.

Disciplinary procedures, triggered off by such misconduct, ought to be fair and reasonable at all times, aiming to correct and enhance performance and behaviour rather than just punishing an errant employee. Try to deal with minor breaches in an informal manner, by talking to the worker to discover the cause(s) of the problem, outlining the standards required, mutually seeking ways to remedy the lapse and so on. A quiet word in the ear often works wonders. If this approach fails, you will have to take disciplinary action which could consist of a formal oral warning followed by a written warning for repeated minor offences or serious misconduct, a final written warning for continued, unsatisfactory conduct and dismissal, as a last resort.

Never forget to act fairly and reasonably, though. Detail your complaint to the employee. Ask for and listen to his or her explanation. Check facts and see both sides of the situation. Make your decision, explaining your reasons, what is expected of him or her and how this can be achieved. Make a note of a warning in your records. Agree to meet again in the near future to review the problem. If it still exists at that stage, contemplate moving on to the next step in the disciplinary process. If it has been remedied, congratulate the worker and remove the note of the warning from the records.

Your **grievance procedure** ought to be fair and reasonable as well. Encourage dissatisfied employees to raise problems with you on an informal basis and do your best to settle them for your mutual benefit. An unhappy person is not going to labour as hard or as well as you would like him or her to do. Be sympathetic, work through the difficulty, listen to his or her comments and ascertain facts prior to making a decision. Don't be afraid to seek external help and guidance to resolve a problem, perhaps agreeing with the aggrieved employee to abide by an outsider's suggestions if you cannot settle a dispute between yourselves. For further reading on these topics, contact your local ACAS office (see page 149) which can provide several free booklets: *Workplace Communications, Disciplinary Practice and Procedures in Employment*, and *Conciliation between Individuals and Employers*.

MOTIVATING A TEAM

Employees of small independent shops are often unmotivated. Pay is fairly meagre, part-time staff may be working mainly to supplement a family income and full-timers see few opportunities for career progression, and in recessionary times are more likely to be concerned about losing their employment. As your success (or failure) is so heavily dependent upon your team, you must think of ways of keeping them satisfied and motivated to work hard and be attentive to your customers.

Pay

You will obviously not wish to pay your staff more than the going rate for retail workers. Nevertheless, it is worth thinking about some form of incentive scheme, whereby bonuses are paid according to results: if sales exceed £2,000 in a week, an extra £20 will be paid to each employee and so on. Set up team rather than individual schemes so that they all benefit equally. This way they pull together rather than fight among themselves for customers. Also, increase pay—possibly in line with inflation—automatically each year, so that resentful and agitated staff do not have to ask you for a rise.

Holidays

Although there will be certain times of the year when you do not want employees to have days or weeks off—Christmas, New Year and so on—try to allow them to pick and choose their holidays outside of these periods. In addition to increasing holiday allowances in line with length of employment, consider offering extra days off for achieving sales targets and so forth.

Welfare facilities

Do ensure that your staff work in a pleasant environment, with space to move about, a room for coffee and lunch breaks and up-to-date equipment to use. Improve team spirit and morale by arranging social events which you, your employees and partners can attend, such as meals at restaurants, visits to the theatre and Christmas parties.

Discounted goods

Most businesses offer their workers cut price goods and services, ranging from ten per cent discounts upwards (perhaps based upon each individual employee's length of service). You also ought to give generous discounts to your team if you wish to retain and build upon their loyalty and goodwill. Selling stock to them at trade prices—with you retaining any prompt payment discounts made available by the suppliers—may be appropriate in some circumstances.

Sick pay schemes

Contemplate handing over more than statutory sickness payments during bouts of sickness, especially as you can reclaim these sums. You might consider linking such a scheme to the employee's length of employment with you—perhaps full pay for the first two weeks of sickness followed by half pay for the next two weeks for employees who have been with you for one year or more, full pay for the first four weeks of sickness and half pay for the following four weeks for those with over two years' employment behind them.

Increased job involvement

Typically, the sales assistants whom you employ will be expected to do a little of everything, from unloading stock deliveries, keeping the shop in order and handling customers. View them as Jacks and Jacquies of all trades rather than general dogsbodies though, if you want to make them feel that they are important to the business. Ask their opinions about their work, allow them to make suggestions and permit them to tackle tasks in their own ways. Even if their approach is different from yours, it may be equally valid and successful.

Personal motivation

You can gee up your staff by having a positive attitude towards them, work and customers at all times. They will take their lead from you. If you treat them badly they are more likely to criticise you behind your back and perhaps even steal from you. Should you lounge about, they will slow down too. If you abuse customers, so will they. So show interest in them, acknowledge their progress, congratulate them when they do well and encourage them when they fail. Work hard, always cleaning, tidying up, rearranging stock and seeking improvements. Deal with customers as you would wish to be handled. Your team will respond in the same, wholehearted manner.

FIRING EMPLOYEES

It is relatively easy to take on staff but, unless they wish to leave, ending their employment may be less straightforward. To handle this task in the proper manner, you should be broadly familiar with the ins and outs of giving notice as well as dismissals and redundancies.

Giving notice

Employees who work for 16 hours or more per week (and those who have been employed for between eight and 16 hours each week for five years) are entitled to minimum periods of notice according to their length of service. After one month's employment, one week's notice must be given and this remains the statutory minimum until two year's employment has been fulfilled. Thereafter, they must receive an additional week's notice for every completed year up a maximum of 12 weeks' notice. In return, employees who have been employed for one month or more must, regardless of their length of service, give one week's notice to their employer.

Of course, these are minimum periods and you may mutually agree to longer terms being incorporated within the written statement of the main terms of employment. Think carefully before doing this though. If you promise to give a longer notice period than is legally necessary, you may have a potentially discontented employee on the premises for that much longer. Should you decide to pay him or her off in lieu of notice, it will cost you that much more. If he or she agrees to giving a lengthier period of notice but then decides to walk out immediately, there is little you can do to stop him or her. It is hardly worthwhile trying to keep him or her to the agreement or to sue for compensation.

Notice can normally be given at any time and does not have to be in writing. The period of notice then commences from the next day. The usual rate of pay applies during this time. If the employee has been with you for six months or more, he or she may request—orally or in writing—a written statement outlining the reason(s) for the dismissal. This must be provided by you within 14 days of such a demand.

There are exceptions to these legal duties and obligations which you ought to know about. Either party may terminate the contract of employment without any notice whatsoever if the (gross) behaviour of the other side warrants it. Also, either party can waive his or her entitlement to notice, should he or she wish to do so. In some instances, both employer and employee may agree that it would be mutually beneficial for the employee to leave immediately. Further information on giving notice may be obtained from the Department of Employment (see page 149) which can provide a useful free booklet called *Rights to Notice and Reasons for Dismissal.*

Dismissals

A dismissal must be 'fair' which means that you should have 'sufficient reason' and ought to have 'acted reasonably' at all times. 'Sufficient reason' might include:

- the employee's inability to do the job properly;
- continual minor or sudden gross misconduct, such as fighting or stealing;
- legal reasons for stopping him or her working, such as a driving ban;
- redundancy, where the job ceases to exist
- or any other 'substantial reason', such as passing trade secrets to a rival.

To 'act reasonably', you must give him or her every chance and assistance to improve, consider the possibilities of alternative employment and not discriminate because of sex, marital status or race.

An 'unfair' dismissal occurs when you do not have a 'fair' reason and/or acted 'unreasonably'. An employee who resigns because you broke one of the main terms of his or her contract—such as cutting pay or hours of work—could also claim he or she was subject to a 'constructive' (and therefore 'unfair') dismissal since your behaviour effectively forced him or her to leave. Anyone who has been employed by you for 16 hours or more per week for two years (or for between eight and 16 hours each week for five years) and who is below retirement age is eligible to bring a claim against you for an 'unfair' dismissal at an **industrial tribunal**. Regardless of service or age, everyone who has been sacked because of their sex, marital status, race or pregnancy may do so too.

Industrial tribunals
You should have no need to encounter these. They are independent judicial bodies set up to settle employment disputes. Seventy-five per cent of cases relate to unfair dismissals although other matters, such as race relations, equal pay and redundancy payments, are dealt with as well. Regarding unfair dismissal, a tribunal may order reinstatement in the job on identical terms and conditions, re-engagement in a similar job, or financial compensation which can run into five-figure sums. The opportunities to appeal against a decision are very limited.

To avoid such a course of action, be fair and reasonable.

- consult your solicitor for advice if necessary.
- explain your reasons for dismissal, to part on as pleasant terms as is possible in the circumstances.
- provide written confirmation on request and give the agreed notice or (probably better) payment in lieu of notice.

Read more on this topic too. The Department of Employment can supply you with *Fair and Unfair Dismissal—A Guide for Employers, The Law on Unfair Dismissal—Guidance for Small Firms* and *Industrial Tribunals Procedure.*

Redundancies

If a job or jobs cease to exist, perhaps because of a sustained slump, you must fulfil your legal duties, should attend to your moral obligations and may have to make redundancy payment(s) too. Legally, you have to select people to be made redundant on a fair basis—'first in, last out' is often used. Those chosen employees who have worked for you for at least 16 hours per week for two years (or for between eight and 16 hours each week for five years) must be given reasonable paid time off to seek new work or retraining opportunities. If ten or more workers are to be made redundant, the Department of Employment ought to be informed.

Redundancy can be extremely traumatic, so morally you should attempt to give those selected as much notice as you can so that they can try to find alternative employment. You should also allow everyone—not just those who are legally entitled to it—reasonable paid time off to secure their futures. Let them use your facilities too—secretarial staff, photocopiers and so on—to help them with typing application letters, photocopying curricula vitae and so forth. Do everything you can to assist them.

Those employees who have been employed by you for 16 hours each week for two years (or for eight to 16 hours per week for five years), and who are below retirement age, may be entitled to a **redundancy payment** from you. The sum due is related to their age, pay and length of service and ranges from half a week's pay to one-and-a-half week's pay per completed year, so it may prove costly. The Department of Employment can supply various useful booklets including: *Procedure for Handling Redundancies, Facing Redundancy: Time Off for Job Hunting or to Arrange Training* and *Redundancy Payments.*

CHECKLIST

1 Do you know how to appraise your staffing needs, consequently attracting, screening, interviewing and offering jobs to quality applicants?

2 Are you familiar with managing a workforce on a face-to-face, daily basis?

3 Do you know of the various ways of motivating shop staff?

4 Have you decided which ones are appropriate to your employees?

5 Are you conversant with the legalities involved with giving notice, dismissals and redundancies?

6 Are you ready to understand shop law?

7
Understanding Law

Legislation will influence many if not all aspects of your retail business. Hence, you should be aware of:

- employment laws
- health and safety laws
- consumer protection laws.

It is also sensible to think about some of the most common legal problems that are faced by retailers on a day-to-day basis, and know the solutions to them.

EMPLOYMENT LAWS

Try to develop a broad understanding of the main points of the key acts, both in theory and through the ways in which they translate into everyday work practices.

The Employment Protection (Consolidation) Act 1978
This act—variously amended and updated in parts by the Employment Acts of 1980, 1982 and 1988—is the cornerstone of employment legislation today. It covers most employment issues of relevance to the small business owner. Although sometimes subject to various qualifying conditions, employees are generally entitled to a written statement of the main terms of employment, itemised pay statements, statutory sick pay, maternity benefits, holidays and time off, statutory periods of notice, a written statement of the reasons for dismissal, redundancy pay and not to be unfairly dismissed.

The Sex Discrimination Act 1975
It is unlawful to discriminate on the grounds of sex or marital status with regard to:

- advertising for staff
- recruiting

- terms and conditions of employment
- facilities and benefits
- training
- transfer
- promotion
- dismissal
- or redundancy

Unlawful discrimination may be termed 'direct' or 'indirect'. **Direct discrimination** takes place when a person is treated less favourably than another of the opposite sex or different marital status would be in the same or similar circumstances. **Indirect discrimination** occurs when requirements or conditions are set which tend to favour people of one sex or marital status more than others.

The act applies to women and men, full and part timers, regardless of their length of employment. No minimum period of employment is required for the act to be effective. Sex discrimination is only lawful if it is a genuine occupational qualification: a person of a particular sex may be needed for authenticity, to preserve privacy or to maintain decency. Other limited exceptions relate to jobs in private households and the armed forces.

The Race Relations Act 1976

It is illegal to discriminate because of colour, race, nationality or ethnic origins in employment matters from recruitment through to dismissal. Again, discrimination can be either direct or indirect by nature. Similarly, selection on racial grounds is only allowed when it is a genuine occupational qualification. Private households and the Civil Service are not covered by this Act.

The Disabled Persons (Employment) Act 1958

Employers with 20 or more workers, which you may have at some stage in the future, have a duty to employ a quota of registered disabled people (as listed at the Jobcentre). In 1992 the quota stands at three per cent of their workforce. It is not an offence to be below quota but those employers who are have a responsibility to take on suitable registered disabled people if they are available when vacancies occur. Should an employer wish to recruit an able bodied person instead, a permit must be obtained from the Jobcentre. Employers with over 20 staff should keep records showing the number and names of employees with starting and finishing dates, clearly identifying registered disabled people in their employment.

The Equal Pay Act 1970

Employees are entitled to equal pay, terms and conditions of employment if the work they do is the same, broadly similar or of equal value to that of other employees. The Act applies to all employees, regardless of their jobs or the number of hours that they work for. The only legitimate exception exists when an employer pays his or her staff higher wages after so many years' service.

Points to consider

What legal matters should I consider when hiring employees?
Avoid discriminating either directly or indirectly because of sex, marital status and/or race. In particular, think about your employee specifications, job advertisements and notices, screening and interview questions as well as your selection criteria. If you employ 20 or more staff, contemplate your responsibilities to registered disabled people. Also, draw up a written statement of the main terms of employment for those recruits who will work for 16 hours or more per week (as well as for those who have worked for eight to 16 hours each week for five years).

What legal issues should I remember when managing a workforce?
These are many and varied and it is advisable to study this topic in immense detail to avoid falling foul of the law. Important issues include:

* discrimination
* equal pay and opportunities
* itemised pay statements
* PAYE
* sickness pay
* maternity benefits
* holidays and time off
* disciplinary and grievance procedures.

You must have a broad and firm grasp of your legal obligations with regard to each topic.

What are my legal responsibilities when ending employment?
You have to be conscious of the statutory periods of notice that must be given, and should act in a fair and reasonable manner when dismissing staff, or making them redundant. At the same time, bear in mind your moral responsibilities by seeing the other party's viewpoint

and doing all you can to help them. When discussing employment law, it is easy to adopt the attitude that 'I'll do as the law states, but no more', yet the more you give, the more you'll receive in return.

What will happen to me if I break any of these employment laws?
In many instances, nothing will happen at all if your employees are unaware of the breach(es). However, you are liable to be taken to an industrial tribunal and could be fined a heavy sum. As significant as this, there might be an enormous amount of adverse publicity about your behaviour which could alienate existing employees, future employees and customers. Don't take risks—play fair at all times.

Where may I obtain more information about employment legislation?
Copies of the various Acts can be purchased from Her Majesty's Stationery Office. The Department of Employment, the Equal Opportunities Commission and the Commission for Racial Equality may provide general and specific advice and guidance geared to your individual situation. Addresses and telephone numbers are on pages 149 and 150.

HEALTH AND SAFETY LAWS

You must take steps to secure and maintain the welfare not only of your employees but also of any visitors to your premises, such as customers and sales representatives. Being aware of and adhering to statutory rules and regulations should help to avoid accidents and the possibilities of being sued by injured persons. Several Acts have been passed in this field, amongst them the Offices, Shops and Railway Premises Act (1963) and the Occupiers Liability Act (1984), but the aptly named **Health and Safety at Work Act** effectively encompasses all of them as far as retailers are concerned.

The Health and Safety at Work Act 1974
Shopkeepers who employ staff must register with their local authority. As far as is reasonably practicable, they then have to provide safe work systems, plant, machinery and equipment plus comfortable working conditions and a secure environment for these employees. Employers who have five or more people working for them need to draw up a written **health and safety statement** outlining their rules and procedures. This has to be kept on display for everyone to see. Sufficient additional information, guidance and supervision must be offered to staff on an ongoing basis so that health and safety standards are upheld. The **Health and Safety Executive** has to be

notified within seven days of any accidents which lead to three or more days' absence from work by any one person. Immediate notification by telephone must be given in the event of serious accidents, loss of eyesight, limbs and so forth—with written confirmation following.

Points to consider
How can I make sure that employees and visitors remain safe and healthy?
Clearly, this depends upon your individual business and premises. Examples of practical steps that you might take include:

- teaching employees how to handle and store goods in the proper manner;
- providing free protective clothing and equipment where necessary;
- showing staff how to use machinery and checking, servicing and repairing it regularly;
- ensuring that passages, stairs and floors are solidly constructed, unobstructed and free from slippery substances such as oil and grease.

Have a fully stocked first aid box on the property, and tell employees where it is and how to use its contents.

How do I make certain that my staff and customers are comfortable whilst on my premises?
Again, circumstances vary but pay attention to:

- heating
- ventilation
- lighting
- catering
- welfare
- washroom facilities.

Don't let employees become too relaxed and comfortable though, otherwise they will not be as industrious as they could be. Try to strike a happy medium.

What else should I be doing with regard to health and safety measures?
Always bear in mind that work situations change and develop over

time so you must forever be monitoring and revising work practices, reminding and reteaching staff and rewriting your written statement, if appropriate. Keep talking to staff, customers and other visitors about ways of continually improving health and safety procedures. Even one accident is one too many.

What do I do if an accident occurs in my shop?
A basic first aid course, perhaps organised though a local school or college on an evening, Saturday or summer school basis, will help. You and your employees would be well advised to attend one. As far as the technicalities are concerned, note down all accidents in an accident book, detailing dates, times, locations, descriptions, action taken and consequences. Tell the Health and Safety Executive about serious accidents either immediately or within seven days, in accordance with the Act.

Who can I approach for more advice on health and safety matters?
Copies of the Health and Safety Act 1974 may be obtained from Her Majesty's Stationery Office. The Health and Safety Executive can provide general advice and useful free leaflets. These include *The Act Outlined—Health and Safety at Work Act 1974* (HSC2), *Writing a Safety Policy Statement: Advice to Employers* (HSC6) and *First Aid Provision in Small Workplaces: Your Questions Answered* (ND [G] 3 [L]). The health and safety inspectors in the environmental health department of your local authority can offer more specific information geared to your situation (addresses and phone numbers are on page 150).

CONSUMER PROTECTION LAWS

Parts of several consumer Acts which have been passed are especially relevant to retailers and their customers. You ought to be broadly aware of these key sections and also need to know the answers to the most common consumer problems which arise from time to time, even in the best run shops.

The Sale of Goods Act 1979
Goods sold must be

- as described
- of merchantable quality
- and fit for a specified purpose

to comply with this Act. 'As described' means that they should match their description. A customer who orders a blue settee from a catalogue must not receive a grey one. 'Of merchantable quality' indicates that they should be fit for their normal purpose. A lawn mower must cut grass. 'Fit for a specified purpose' suggests that they should be suitable for any purpose specified by a customer before the sale and agreed with by the retailer. If a customer asks whether a tube of glue can be used for sticking a heel back onto a shoe and the retailer confirms that it is, then that glue must perform the task satisfactorily.

The Supply of Goods (Implied Terms) Act 1973
The Sale of Goods Act always applies to transactions between a retailer and his or her customers. The use of notices and signs which contain exclusion clauses such as 'No refunds can be given under any circumstances whatsoever' cannot take away any of the customers' statutory rights. Furthermore, it is a criminal offence to display these notices and signs.

The Supply of Goods and Services Act 1982
Retailers who provide services such as repairing products must complete their work with reasonable skill, using materials of suitable quality. A faulty midi-system should be repaired with parts which are manufactured for that particular product. Retailers also have a duty to take reasonable care of any goods in their possession and ought to carry out services and repairs within a reasonable time, given the amount of work involved in each individual task.

The Unfair Contract Terms Act 1977
Exclusion clauses which attempt to excuse liability for personal injury and/or death, either in contracts or by notices given or displayed, are illegal. Those concerning other losses such as to property are only valid if they are deemed to be reasonable.

The Trade Descriptions Act 1972
Retailers must not falsely describe, make false statements or supply misleading information about their products or services. All descriptions—verbal and written—have to be truthful and accurate. 'Handmade' goods ought to be made by hand. 'Twenty-four-hour photo processing' should mean that a customer's photographs are ready within 24 hours. Retailers must not compare their prices to a manufacturer's so called 'recommended prices'. Neither should they

make false comparisons between current sale and former prices. Unless clearly stated, the old price ought to have been charged for at least 28 days in the previous six months.

The Consumer Act 1987
Certain goods have to comply with specific safety requirements designed to cover potentially dangerous items such as electrical appliances and toys. Also, producers—including retailers who import products from around the world and sell them as their own—are liable if these goods are defective and cause damage to property exceeding £275 and/or personal injury and/or death to anyone.

The Unsolicited Goods and Services Act 1971
Customers are not obliged to pay for products or services which they did not order. Retailers who send out products hoping that they will be purchased (inertia selling) can be fined if they forward an invoice, demand payment or threaten legal action regarding their unsolicited goods. If the products remain uncollected for six months, they become the property of the customer. This six-month period may be shortened to only 30 days if the customer writes to the retailer requesting collection within the shorter period.

Questions and answers
Do these consumer Acts apply to all of my goods?
Yes, they apply to any products which are sold by you to your customers, including sale and secondhand items. They also cover goods that are rented out or are subject to credit agreements.

Am I legally obliged to sell my stock to a customer?
No, a customer cannot force you to make a sale against your wishes. By displaying stock, you are simply inviting offers which you are free to accept or reject. For example, you may decline an offer because you have mispriced an item or do not want to rearrange a display. Be careful though; if you refuse a sale because you have underpriced goods, you could be accused of breaching the Trade Descriptions Act by providing false or misleading information on a display.

Do I have to refund a deposit to a customer who cancels an order?
Generally speaking, no. By handing over and accepting a deposit, your customer and you have entered into a legally binding agreement whereby you supply goods in return for payment. If you fulfil your obligation within a reasonable or the agreed time, you are entitled to

the deposit and the balance too.

Do I have to give a receipt for every sale?
No, but it would be extremely naïve not to do so. You may find it will cause problems later on if a product is brought back by a customer.

Am I legally obliged to accept goods returned to me by a dissatisfied customer?
No, if he or she has just taken a dislike to them. Yes, if they are faulty, unless:

- the customer used the products contrary to your specific advice and damaged them as a result of this;
- a person other than the customer returns them to you. Your contract is with the customer, not the recipient of a gift of the goods.

Does a customer have to produce a receipt to bring back faulty items?
No, he or she is legally entitled to return them even without the receipt, the wrapping or the bag. He or she does need to prove in some way that they were bought from your shop though (which is why you should always issue receipts).

Do I have to make a full refund for faulty goods?
Yes, although you can ask the customer to accept an exchange or a credit note for later use. He or she makes the final decision though.

Can a customer claim damages resulting from faulty products?
Yes, he or she may demand compensation from you if they cause damage to person or property and can also claim expenses for contacting you and returning them to the shop.

Does a manufacturer's guarantee affect cusomers' right?
No, not at all. It should simply be regarded as a bonus for the customer, over and above his or her statutory rights. Your responsibilities to your customers remain the same.

May I return faulty items to my suppliers?
In most cases, yes. You have the same basic rights with your suppliers as your customers do with you. Any contract of sale which seeks to restrict or remove any of these rights must be reasonable if it is to be valid.

What do I do with uncollected items, left with me for repair or service?
After a reasonable period of time, you can send a letter by recorded
delivery to the customer, telling him or her that you will sell the goods
to pay for any work and costs if they are not collected. At least three
months' notice must be given, at which stage a sale can take place.
Costs can be deducted and any remaining balance forwarded to the
customer. If you cannot contact the customer, you must not sell the
items and must take reasonable care of them whilst they are in your
possession.

What will happen if I break the law?
In these instances, you may be sued for a refund, damages and costs
(as appropriate) by a customer, perhaps via the courts. Negative,
word of mouth comments amongst his or her friends and colleagues
plus possible media coverage make this essential to avoid. In extreme
cases, the Trading Standards Officer of the council could initiate
proceedings against you.

'About that kitten you sold me...'

Where can I find out more about consumer protection issues?
Copies of the different Acts can be purchased from Her Majesty's
Stationery Office. The Office of Fair Trading, the British Standards
Institute and the Trading Standards Officer of your local authority

may provide assistance too (see page 150 for addresses and telephone numbers).

STATUTES CHECKLIST

- The Employment Protection (Consolidation) Act 1978
- The Sex Discrimination Act 1975
- The Race Relations Act 1976
- The Disabled Persons (Employment) Act 1958
- The Equal Pay Act 1970
- The Health and Safety at Work Act 1974
- The Sale of Goods Act 1979
- The Supply of Goods (Implied Terms) Act 1973
- The Supply of Goods and Services Act 1982
- The Unfair Contracts Terms Act 1977
- The Trade Description Act 1972
- The Consumer Act 1977
- The Unsolicited Goods and Services Act 1971

CHECKLIST

1 Are you familiar with the main terms of the key employment laws?

2 Do you know the answers to the most common employment questions?

3 Are you conversant with health and safety legislation?

4 Do you know how the law operates in practice?

5 Are you aware of the various consumer protection laws that may affect you?

6 Do you know how these work on a day-to-day basis?

7 Are you ready to face the future?

8
Facing the Future

With a combination of skill, hard work and good fortune, you may create a successful shop. You may never become rich but the satisfaction of running a business and reaching your own decisions is much more important, as every self-employed retailer will tell you. At some stage, you will then decide to expand to larger premises or to start or buy a second retail outlet. The key to continued success is to review the past. This will enable you to win again and again in the future.

INTRODUCING RETAILING

- You should now possess a hands-on knowledge of your trade. Do you really want to continue working within it? Think of changing trades if you are unhappy.

- Consider the pluses and minuses of shopkeeping as you see them. Do the advantages truly outweigh the disadvantages? The long hours, mental stress and financial risks will all increase if you expand.

- Decide whether you have the qualities needed to be your own boss in the retail trade. Are your family still as supportive? They will see less of you and be under more financial strain from now on. Are your goals realistic? Don't run before you have learned to walk properly.

- Contemplate the benefits and drawbacks of operating as a sole proprietor, partnership and franchisee. Is it time to change? Perhaps you need to take in partners to raise funds or to broaden expertise. If so, remember you'll need to sign a partnership agreement.

- Continue to seek advice from experienced individuals and

organisations. Who has been most helpful to you so far? Refer to the Small Firms Service or whoever when you want a second opinion.

RAISING FINANCE

- Think about where you may obtain finance for expansion. Can you now use more of your own money? Weigh up the positive and negative aspects of self versus borrowed funding.

- Decide whether you require a loan, overdraft and/or commercial mortgage. Which is most suited to your needs? Bear in mind that you now have a track record and may offer a going concern as security, so any borrowings should be on better terms than before.

- Carry on using your business plan to monitor your performance, updating profit budgets and cashflow forecasts each month. How accurate were your original predictions? Draw up a new plan based on the extensive experience you now have.

- Discuss funding with a prospective lender. Are you satisfied with your bank? Be prepared to transfer if you are not receiving the service that you require.

STARTING UP

- Be ready for another lengthy search over a wide area before you come across a second suitable opportunity. Can you be patient for perhaps a year or so until your chance arises? Again, apply your selection criteria concerning location, neighbours, surroundings and competitors to all opportunities.

- Assess vacant premises or going concerns along previous lines, seeking independent valuations and negotiating hard before signing any legally binding document. Have you learned from any earlier mistakes? Back out of a deal if you feel it isn't perfect for you.

- You now know how to make a shop look attractive, both externally and internally. Should you model a new outlet upon the existing one, or make changes? Don't forget to secure your property against burglars and shoplifters.

- Carry on appraising your suppliers and stock to ensure that they are right for you. Should you continue with them in your next shop? Perhaps it would be more appropriate to move up- or downmarket according to the circumstances.

- Renew your various insurance policies. Have you been caught without insurance at any time? Extend and add to your insurance arrangements to take account of developing situations.

- Maintain a checklist of miscellaneous dos and don'ts. Do you always forget to re-order cheque books or to refill the first aid box? You'll be twice as forgetful with that second unit.

KEEPING RECORDS

- Continue to detail information into your various books, lists and files. Are you doing this on a daily, weekly and monthly basis? Keeping control is even more important when you begin to expand.

- Compile trading accounts, profit and loss accounts and balance sheets at quarterly intervals. Is your accountant drawing together annual accounts on your behalf? Don't be too mean to pay the fees—he or she knows the ropes, unlike you.

- Constantly analyse your accounts to see how well your business is trading. Are you familiar with the different ratios that can be used? Theoretical though they may seem, they are rough and ready measures of success.

- Stay up to date with Income Tax, Value Added Tax and National Insurance payments. Have you fallen behind because the authorities haven't chased you? Be conscious of the changes involved with expansion, such as PAYE and National Insurance Contributions for extra staff.

MARKETING YOURSELF

- Go on researching your marketplace, particularly your products, customers and competitors and their effects upon your business. Are you acting before instead of reacting after market changes? Be aware that your second shop—perhaps upmarket and in a different location—could effectively be operating in another marketplace.

- Maintain a close watch on your prices at all times. Do you have a flexible pricing structure? By purchasing more goods for two stores, you should obtain greater discounts which may allow you to improve your prices.

- However well you are doing, continue to promote your venture to the right people at minimal expense. Do you know which advertising approaches are successful for you? Window displays, leaflets, letters, press releases and word of mouth should help your second outlet to succeed as well.

- You should now have developed that sixth sense needed to deal with customers on a face-to-face basis. Are all of the people coming into your shop buying from you? Keep striving to make a sale on each and every occasion.

EMPLOYING STAFF

- Carry on assessing your needs, attracting, screening and interviewing job applicants in a proper manner. Are you recruiting quality staff? Bear in mind that different types of employee may now be required, such as a manager for your first shop.

- Stay in control of managing your workforce as you expand. Do you feel you are a successful manager? Contemplate allocating some responsibilities and tasks to a trusted second-in-command.

- Keep on trying to motivate your team. Are you helping to make them dynamic self-starters? Don't forget there are several motivating factors other than pay that are worth careful consideration.

- Be prepared to dismiss staff when necessary. Are you acting fairly? Do you have sufficient reason to fire them? Be aware of your obligations when giving notice.

UNDERSTANDING LAW

- You should now be familiar with the key employment laws. Do you keep up to date with changing legislation in this field? Be conscious of how increasing numbers of employees affect your legal obligations to your workforce.

- Make sure that you look after the health and safety of your staff (and customers). Are you always seeking ways to improve their working conditions? Keep talking, and listening to sensible suggestions from them.

- Stay aware of the leading consumer protection laws and how these influence customer relations. Do you treat customers in a fair and even-handed manner? Never forget that they are your business. You cannot survive without them.

CHECKLIST

1 Have you had a complete introduction to the retail trade?

2 Do you know how to raise finance for your firm?

3 Are you able to start a successful business from scratch or buy a winning concern?

4 Do you understand how to keep records?

5 Are you able to market yourself properly?

6 Do you know how to employ staff?

7 Do you understand employment, health and safety and consumer protection laws?

Glossary

Annual accounts. Formal statements showing the financial position of a business, which are normally drawn up by an accountant and submitted to the Inland Revenue for tax assessment purposes. They usually comprise a trading account, a profit and loss account and a balance sheet.

Anticipated sales. Expected sums of money to be received over a future period of time.

Cash on collection. A trading term whereby cash must be paid when goods are collected from a supplier.

Cash on delivery. A trading term whereby cash has to be paid when items are delivered to a buyer.

Clauses. Sections of an agreement such as a lease, detailing terms and conditions.

Cost of sales. A sum calculated by taking initial stock, adding stock purchases and deducting remaining stock over a given period.

Counter. A unit on which a cash register is placed, ideally with additional space beneath to store miscellaneous items such as a dustpan and brush, first aid kit, fire extinguisher and carrier bags.

Credit facilities. The business practice of allowing a customer to pay for goods and services at a later date, typically 30 days in the retail trade.

Current assets. Constantly changing items owned or owed to a business such as stock, debts and cash in hand, as noted on a balance sheet.

Current liabilities. Short term business debts to perhaps banks and suppliers, as detailed on a balance sheet.

Direct discrimination. This exists when one person is treated less favourably than another is or would be treated in the same or similar circumstances, usually because of his or her sex, marital status or race.

Disciplinary rules. Guidelines setting out the required standards of work performance and behaviour expected of employees.

Disciplinary procedures. Steps which employers should follow when

135

investigating breaches of disciplinary rules.

Draft contract. A provisional and legally unbinding document drawn up by one party for the approval of and possible amendment by another party.

Enterprise Allowance Scheme. A Government devised scheme whereby individuals who stop drawing unemployment benefit to start a business are entitled to financial and advisory assistance in the early days of the venture.

Expiry of a lease. The period of time when the leasehold agreement has ended, although **renewal** of the lease may occur, subject to various excpetions.

Financed by. An accounting term indicating how business activities over a particular period have been funded, usually by capital and loan facilities.

Fixed assets. Items of long term use to a business such as a freehold property, fixtures and fittings.

Fixed interest rates. Those rates which are set when funding is arranged and do not vary for a given period.

Franchise. A licence for one party to set up and run a venture in a particular area for a specific period of time, using the trading name and business format of another party.

Franchisee. The party buying a franchise. (The party granting the franchise is known as a franchisor.)

From scratch. A slang expression commonly used to describe a business which has been or will be created from nothing—the entrepreneur must find, design and layout premises, fill them with goods and so on.

Full repairing and insuring liability. A legal obligation whereby the tenant of a property is responsible for its internal and external maintenance and insurance.

Full timers. Staff who are employed for approximately 35 to 40 hours per week (although in the eyes of the law, anyone working for more than 16 hours each week is usually entitled to the same employment rights).

Going concern. A well established business which appears to be trading satisfactorily (although an examination of its books and accounts may convey a different and more accurate image).

Goods owed. Outstanding items due to be handed over to one party by another.

Grievance procedures. Steps which employers and employees should adhere to when dealing with employees' complaints.

Gross profit. The profit derived from buying and selling goods and services, before the deduction of overheads such as rent, wages and transport costs.

Health and safety statement. A legal document outlining health and safety rules and procedures, drawn up and displayed by employers with five or more employees.

Indirect discrimination. This exists when terms and conditions are set which favour one group of people more than another, usually because of their sex, marital status or race.

Industrial tribunals. Independent and informal judicial bodies established to deal with employment disputes, mainly involving (alleged) unfair dismissals.

Input tax. Value added tax charged on products and services purchased by a VAT registered trader for resale or business use.

Internal repairing liability. A legal obligation whereby the occupant of a property is responsible for its internal repairs and maintenance.

Job description. A written summary of the title, purpose and tasks of a job.

Job title. A self explanatory name used to describe a job. Ideally, it should be short and to the point.

Loan Guarantee Scheme. A Government backed scheme whereby entrepreneurs with a viable business idea but insufficient funds can borrow money which is (partly) secured by the Government.

Losses. Deficits occurring when costs exceed sales revenue.

Monies owed. Outstanding sums due to be paid by one party to another.

Net assets. The total of **net current assets** added to **fixed assets**.

Output tax. Value added tax charged by a VAT registered trader on goods and services sold to customers.

Overheads. Costs incurred by a business regardless of its sales turnover.

Personal drawings. Monies taken out of a business for personal use, as noted on the balance sheet.

Premium. A sum of money paid to the existing tenant of a leasehold property in order to acquire his or her lease.

Profit budget. A statement of anticipated sales, overheads and profits or losses over a given period, typically one year.

Profits. The amount remaining after costs have been deducted from sales revenue.

Redundancy payment. A sum of money paid to redundant employees according to age, pay and length of service, subject to various qualifying conditions.

Renewal of a lease. A period of time when a lease has expired and the existing tenant is usually entitled to another lease on the same terms and conditions.

Part timers. Employees who work for up to 16 hours per week. (Those who are employed for more than 16 hours enjoy the same employment benefits as full timers.)

Partnership. A legally binding business association of two to 20 people. Each partner is usually equally liable for all of the partnership's debts.

Pay as You Earn (PAYE). A scheme whereby employers have to deduct tax and national insurance from employees' wages to pass them to the Inland Revenue each month.

Rent reviews. Pre-agreed times within a leasehold agreement whereby the existing rent is appraised and amended in line with current market conditions.

Sale or return. A trading condition whereby unsold stock is returned to the supplier for a cash refund or credit against future purchases.

Sales. Sum total of monies received from goods and services sold over a specific period of time.

Schedule of condition. A legal statement outlining the precise condition of a property at a given time.

Security. Assets pledged by a borrower against monies borrowed, to protect the lender against defaults by the borrower.

Secured borrowings. Loans, overdrafts, mortgages and other financial advances against which assets have been set by a borrower.

Sole proprietor. A person who owns and controls a business alone.

Statutory maternity pay (SMP). A state scheme whereby sums are paid to pregnant employees for up to 18 weeks, subject to qualifying terms and conditions.

Statutory sickness pay (SSP). A State scheme whereby weekly sums are paid to sick employees for up to 28 weeks of illness, subject to qualifying terms and conditions.

Stock. Finished items which are ready to be sold to customers.

Surcharges. Fines levied by HM Customs and Excise on registered traders who have repeatedly not submitted their vat returns and settled ther vat bills on the due dates.

Temporary staff. Those people who are employed on an occasional basis to cater for changing demands.

Trading period. A timespan for which accounts are drawn up, usually 12 months.

Unsecured borrowing. Loans, ovedrafts, mortgages and similar financial advances against which no assets have been pledged by the borrower.

Variable interest rates. Those rates which fluctuate from time to time according to prevailing market conditions.

Window display. A mix of complementary and coordinating goods within a common theme, used to attract customers into the shop.

Further Reading

INTRODUCING RETAILING

Choosing and Using Professional Advisers, P. Chaplin (Kogan Page, London, 1986).

Franchising: A Practical Guide for Franchisors and Franchisees, I. Maitland (Mercury, London 1991).

Handbook of Retailing, A. R. West (Gower, Aldershot, 1988).

RAISING FINANCE

Cashflow and Credit Management, V. Hawkes and K. Slater (Kogan Page, London, 1988).

How to Raise Business Finance, P. Ibbetson (How to Books, Plymouth, 1987).

The Business Planner, I. Maitland (Butterworth Heinemann, Oxford, 1992).

How to Deal with Your Bank Manager, G. Sales (Kogan Page, London, 1988).

The Business Writing Handbook, I. Stewart (Kogan Page, London, 1987).

STARTING UP

Buying a Business, M. Allen and R. Hodgkinson (Graham and Trotman, London, 1988).

Buying for Business, T. Attwood (Kogan Page, London, 1988).

The Small Business Guide, 3rd Edition, C. Barrow (BBC Publications, London, 1988).

How to Choose Business Premises, H. Green, B. Chalkley and P. Foley (Kogan Page, London, 1986).

Security Manual, 5th Edition, E. Oliver and J. Wilson (Gower, Aldershot, 1988).

Bargaining for Results, J. Winkler (Butterworth Heinemann, Oxford, 1989).

KEEPING RECORDS

Financial Management for the Small Business, 2nd edition, C. Barrow (Kogan Page, London, 1988).

How to Master Book-keeping, P. Marshall (How To Books, Plymouth, 1992).

Understand Your Accounts, A. St John Price (Kogan Page, London, 1991).

MARKETING YOURSELF

The Secrets of Successful Selling, T. Adam (Butterworth Heinemann, Oxford, 1986).

The Secrets of Successful Public Relations and Image Making, T. Greener (Butterworth Heinemann, Oxford, 1991).

Do Your Own Market Research, P. Hague and P. Jackson (Kogan Page, London, 1987).

Running a Successful Advertising Campaign, I. Maitland (Telegraph Publications, 1989).

Pricing for Results, J. Winkler (Butterworth Heinemann, Oxford, 1989).

EMPLOYING STAFF

How to Manage People at Work, J. Humphries (How To Books, Plymouth, 1992).

The Barclays' Guide to Managing Staff for the Small Business, I. Maitland (Blackwell, Oxford, 1991).

How to Recruit, I. Maitland (Gower, Aldershot, 1991).

Motivational Leadership, A. Tack (Gower, Aldershot, 1984).

UNDERSTANDING LAW

Law for the Small Business, 6th Edition, P. Clayton (Kogan Page, London, 1988).

Janner's Personnel Law, G. Janner (Gower, Aldershot, 1991).

Business Law, R. G. Lawson and A. A. Painter (Butterworth Heinemann, Oxford, 1989).

FACING THE FUTURE

Sources of Free Business Information, M. J. Brooks (Kogan Page, London, 1988).

The Entrepreneur's Complete Self Assessment Guide, D. A. Gray (Kogan Page, London, 1987).

Going for Growth, M. K. Lawson (Kogan Page, London, 1987).

Managing Change, R. Plant (Gower, Aldershot, 1987).

Useful Addresses

INTRODUCING RETAILING

Alliance of Independent Retailers, Newton Road, Worcester WR5 1JX. Tel: (0905) 28165.

Alliance of Small Firms and Self-Employed People Ltd, 33 The Greene, Calne, Wiltshire SN11 8DJ. Tel: (0249) 817003.

Association of British Chambers of Commerce, Tufton Street, London SW1P 3QB. Tel: (071) 222 1555.

British Franchise Association, Thames View, Newton Road, Henley on Thames, Oxfordshire RG9 1HG. Tel: (0491) 578049.

Business in the Community, 227a City Road, London EC1V 1LX. Tel: (071) 253 3716.

CBD Research Ltd, 15 Wickham Road, Beckenham, Kent BR3 2JS. Tel: (081) 650 7745.

Chartered Association of Certified Accountants, 29 Lincoln's Inn Fields, London WC2A 3EE. Tel: (071) 242 6855.

Institute of Chartered Accountants (England and Wales), Chartered Accountants Hall, PO Box 433, Moorgate Place, London EC2R 6EQ. Tel: (071) 628 7060.

Institute of Chartered Accountants in Ireland, Chartered Accountants House, 87-89 Pembroke Road, Dublin. Tel: (010) 3531 680400.

Institute of Chartered Accountants of Scotland, 27 Queen Street, Edinburgh EH2 1IA. Tel: (031) 225 5673.

Law Society (England and Wales), 113 Chancery Lane, London WC2A 1PL. Tel: (071) 242 1222.

Law Society of Northern Ireland, 90-106 Victoria Street, Belfast BT1 2BJ. Tel: (0232) 231614.

Law Society of Scotland, 26 Drumsheugh Gardens, Edinburgh EH3 7YR. Tel: (031) 226 7411.

National Association of Shopkeepers, 91 Mansfield Road, Nottingham NG1 3FN. Tel: (0642) 475046.

National Chamber of Trade, Enterprise House, 59 Castle Street, Reading, Berkshire RG1 7SN. Tel: (0734) 566744.

National Federation of Self Employed and Small Businesses, 32 St Annes Road West, Lytham St Annes, Lancashire FY8 1NY. Tel: (0253) 720911. And at:

Unit 101c Argent Centre, 60 Frederick Street, Birmingham B1 3HB. Tel: (021) 236 6849.

11 Great George Street, Bristol, Avon BS1 5QY. Tel: (0272) 276073.

Duke Street, Arcade Chambers, Duke Street Arcade, Cardiff CF1 2BA. Tel: (0222) 398640.

34 Argyle Street, Glasgow G2 8BD. Tel: (041) 221 0775.

35a Appletongate, Newark, Nottinghamshire NG24 1JR. Tel: (0636) 701311.

5 Norden House, 39-41 Stowell Street, Newcastle upon Tyne NE1 4YB. Tel: (0632) 324221.

Rural Development Commission, 11 Cowley Street, London SW1P 3NA. Tel: (071) 276 6969.

Small Business Bureau, 32 Smith Square, London SW1P 3HH. Tel: (071) 222 0330.

RAISING FINANCE

Abbey National plc, Abbey House, Baker Street, London NW1 6XL. Tel: (071) 486 5555.

Barclays Bank plc, 54 Lombard Street, London EC3P 3AH. Tel: (071) 626 1567.

Co-operative Bank plc, 1 Balloon Street, Manchester M60 4EP. Tel: (061) 832 3456.

Lloyds Bank plc, 71 Lombard Street, London EC3P 3BS. Tel: (071) 626 1500.

Midland Bank plc, Griffin House, Pennine Centre, 41 Silver Street Head, Sheffield S2 3GG. Tel: (0742) 752394.

National Westminster Bank plc, 8 Fenchurch Place, London EC3M 4PB. Tel: (071) 374 3374.

Nationwide Anglia Building Society, Chesterfield Road, Bloomsbury Way, London WC1V 6PW. Tel: (071) 242 8822.

STARTING UP

Access, Essex House, Southchurch Avenue, Southend on Sea, Essex SS99 3PP. Tel: (0702) 353355.

American Express, PO Box 63, Brighton, Sussex BN1 1YZ. Tel: (0273) 696933.

Association for the Prevention of Theft in Shops, 6-7 Buckingham Street, London WC2N 6BU. Tel: (071) 839 6614.

Barclaycard, PO Box 28, Liverpool L32 8UY. Tel: (051) 473 2500.

British Insurance and Investment Brokers Association, 14 Bevis Marks, London EC3A 7NT. Tel: (071) 623 9043.

Institution of Business Agents, 9 Shirley Road, Acocks Green, Birmingham B27 7XU. Tel: (021) 707 8800.

National Association of Estate Agents, 21 Jury Street, Warwick CV34 3EH. Tel: (0926) 496800.

National Association of Shopfitters, 411 Limpsfield Road, The Green, Upper Warlingham, Surrey CR3 9HA. Tel: (0883) 624961.

Royal Institution of Chartered Surveyors, 12 Great George Street, London SW1P 3AD. Tel: (071) 222 7000.

Shop and Display Equipment Association, 24 Croydon Road, Caterham, Surrey CR3 6YR. Tel: (0883) 348911.

KEEPING RECORDS

Customs and Excise, Alexander House, 21 Victoria Avenue, Southend on Sea, Essex SS99 1AA. Tel: (0702) 348944.

DSS Leaflet Unit, PO Box 21, Stanmore, Middlesex HA7 1AY. Tel: (0800) 393 539.

Inland Revenue, Somerset House, Strand, London WC2R 1LB. Tel: (071) 438 6622.

MARKETING YOURSELF

Advertising Association, Abford House, 15 Wilton Road, London SW1V 1NJ. Tel: (071) 828 2771.

Association of Illustrators, 1 Colville Place, London W1P 1HN. Tel: (071) 636 4100.

British Institute of Professional Photography, 2 Amwell End, Ware, Hertfordshire SG12 9HN. Tel: (0920) 464011.

British Printing Industries Federation, 11 Bedford Row, London WC1R 4DX. Te: (071) 242 6904.

Institute of Marketing, Moor Hall, Cookham, Maidenhead, Berkshire SL6 9HQ. Tel: (06285) 24922.

Institute of Public Relations, 1 Great James Street, London WC1N 3DA. Tel: (071) 405 5505.

Master Photographers Association, Hallmark House, 97 East Street, Epsom, Surrey KT17 1EA. Tel: (0372) 726123.

Society of Typographic Designers, 21-27 Seagrave Road, London SW6 1RP. Tel: (071) 381 4258.

EMPLOYING STAFF

ACAS, 11-12 St James Square, London SW1Y 4LA. Tel: (071) 210 3000. And at:

Alpha Tower, Suffolk Street, Queensway, Birmingham B1 1TZ. Tel: (021) 643 9911.

16 Park Place, Clifton, Bristol, Avon BS8 1JP. Tel: (0272) 211921.

Phase 1, Ty Glas Road, Llanishen, Cardiff CR4 5PH. Tel: (0222) 762636.

Franborough House, 123 Bothwell Street, Glasgow G2 7JR. Tel: (041) 204 2677.

Commerce House, St Albans Place, Leeds, Yorkshire LS2 8HH. Tel: (0532) 431371.

Clifton House, 83 Euston Road, London NW1 2RB. Tel: (071) 388 5100.

Boulton House, 17 Chorlton Street, Manchester M1 3HY. Tel: (061) 228 3222.

Westgate House, Westgate Road, Newcastle on Tyne NE1 1TJ. Tel: (0632) 612191.

Department of Employment, Caxton House, Tothill Street, London SW1H 9NF. Tel: (071) 273 3000.

UNDERSTANDING LAW

British Standards Institution, 2 Park Street, London W1A 2BS. Tel: (071) 629 9000.

Commission for Racial Equality, Elliot House, 10-12 Allington Street, London SW1E 5EH. Tel: (071) 828 7022.

Equal Opportunities Commission, Quay Street, Manchester M3 3HN. Tel: (061) 833 9244. And at:

　　Caerways House, Windsor Lane, Cardiff CF1 1LB. Tel: (0222) 743552.

　　St Andrews House, 141 West Rile Street, Glasgow G1 2RN. Tel: (041) 332 8018.

Health and Safety Executive, St Hugh's House, Trinity Road, Bootle, Merseyside L20 2QY. Tel: (051) 951 4381.

　　Baynards House, 1 Chepstow Place, London W2 4TC. Tel: (071) 229 3456.

　　Broad Lane, Sheffield, Yorkshire S3 7HQ. Tel: (0742) 892345.

Her Majesty's Stationery Office, 51 Nine Elms Lane, London SW8 5DR. Tel: (071) 873 0011.

Office of Fair Trading, Field House, Breams Buildings, London EC4 1PR. Tel: (071) 242 2858.

FACING THE FUTURE

Small Firms Service, Alpha Tower, Suffolk Street, Queensway, Birmingham B1 1TT. (Dial 100, ask for 'Freefone Enterprise'). And at:

　　6th Floor, The Pithay, Bristol, Avon BS1 2NB. ('Freefone Enterprise').

　　Carlyle House, Carlyle Road, Cambridge CB4 3DN. ('Freefone Enterprise').

　　16 St David's House, Wood Street, Cardiff CF1 1ER. ('Freefone Enterprise').

　　21 Bothwell Street, Glasgow G2 6NR. ('Freefone Enterprise').

1 Park Row, City Square, Leeds, Yorkshire LS1 5NR. ('Freefone Enterprise').

Graeme House, Derby Square, Liverpool L2 7UJ. ('Freefone Enterprise').

Ebury Bridge House, 2-18 Ebury Bridge Road, London SW1W 8QD. ('Freefone Enterprise').

3rd Floor, Royal Exchange Buildings, St Ann's Square, Manchester M2 7AH. ('Freefone Enterprise').

Centro House, 3 Cloth Market, Newcastle upon Tyne NE1 1EE. ('Freefone Enterprise').

Severns House, 20 Middle Pavement, Nottingham NG1 7DW. ('Freefone Enterprise').

Abbey Hall, Abbey Square, Reading, Berkshire RG1 3BE. ('Freefone Enterprise').

Please bear in mind that organisations can, and frequently do, relocate and change their phone numbers. You may need to refer to the latest local telephone directory or to dial '192' for directory enquiries.

Index

How to Start a Business from Home
Graham Jones
Second Edition

Most people have dreamed of starting their own business from home at some time or other; but how do you begin? What special skills do you need? This great value-for-money paperback has the answers, showing how you can profit from your own talents and experience, and start turning spare time into cash from the comfort of your own home. *How to Start a Business From Home* contains a wealth of ideas, projects, tips, facts, checklists and quick-reference information for everyone—whether in between jobs, taking early retirement, or students and others with time to invest. Packed with information on everything from choosing a good business idea and starting up to advertising, book-keeping and dealing with professionals, this book is essential reading for every budding entrepreneur.

'Full of ideas and advice.' *The Daily Mirror*. 'Full of excellent practical advice...Essential reading for anyone about to start their own home-based business.' *OwnBase*. 'Packed with details and helpful advice.' *In Business Now (DTI)*.

Graham Jones BSc(Hons) is an editor, journalist and lecturer specialising in practical business subjects. His other books include *Fit to Manage* and *The Business of Freelancing*.
176pp, 1 85703 012 5.

How to Do Your Own Advertising
Michael Bennie

'Entrepreneurs and small businesses are flooding the market with new products and services; the only way to beat the competition is successful selling—and that means advertising.' But what can you afford? This book is for anyone who needs—or wants—to advertise effectively, but does not want to pay agency rates. This book shows you step-by-step how to assemble a simple, straightforward, yet highly successful ad or brochure with the minimum of outside help. Every step is clearly explained with the beginner in mind. There are numerous illustrations, lots of examples of actual ads, a variety of case studies to show the principles in practice and the aim throughout is to make advertising easy and enjoyable. Michael Bennie has had many years' professional experience as a Sales Manager with a number of international companies, covering all aspects of sales and copywriting. He is now a freelance copywriter and advertising consultant, and Director of Studies at the Copywriting School.
176pp illus. 0 7463 0579 6.

How to Keep Business Accounts
Peter Taylor
Second Edition

A new revised edition of an easy-to-understand handbook for all business owners and managers.

> 'Will help you sort out the best way to carry out double entry book-keeping, as well as providing a clear step-by-step guide to accounting procedures.' *Mind Your Own Business*. ' Progresses through the steps to be taken to maintain an effective double entry book-keeping system with the minimum of bother.' *The Accounting Technician*. 'Compulsory reading.' *Manager, National Westminster Bank (Midlands)*.

Peter Taylor is a Fellow of the Institute of Chartered Accountants, and of the Chartered Association of Certified Accountants. He has many years' practical experience of advising small businesses.
176pp illus. 0 7643 0618.0.

How to Master Book-Keeping
Peter Marshall

Book-keeping can seem a confusing subject for people coming to it for the first time. This very clear book will be welcomed by everyone wanting a really user-friendly guide to recording business transactions step-by-step. Illustrated at every stage with specimen entries, the book will also be an ideal companion for students taking LCCI, RSA, BTEC, accountancy technician and similar courses at schools, colleges or training centres. Typical business transactions are used to illustrate all the essential theory, practice and skills required to be effective in a real business setting. Contents: Preface, introduction, theory of double entry, day books, cash book, bank reconciliation, petty cash book, journal, postage book, the ledger, discounts, control accounts, trial balance, accruals and prepayments, revenue accounts, the balance sheet, manufacturing accounts, depreciation, bad and doubtful debts, partnership and accounts, amalgamation of sole proprietorships into a partnership, limited companies, 'going limited', reflection, club accounts, asset disposals, correction of errors, VAT accounts, incomplete records, interpretation of accounts, wages, stock records. Peter Marshall BSc(Econ) BA(Hons) FRSA FSTB MBIM has been Tutor in Education at the University of Lancaster and Director of Studies at the Careers College, Cardiff. He has contributed regularly to *FOCUS on Business Education*.
192pp illus. 1 85703 022 2

How to Employ & Manage Staff
Wendy Wyatt

This easy to use handbook will help all managers and supervisors whose work involves them in recruiting and managing staff. Ideal for quick reference, it provides a ready-made framework of modern employment practice from recruitment onwards. It provides a clear account of how to apply the health & safety at work regulations, how to handle record-keeping, staff development, grievance and disciplinary procedures, maternity and sick leave and similar matters for the benefit of the organisation and its employees. The book includes a useful summary of current employment legislation and is complete with a range of model forms, letters, notices and similar documents. Wendy Wyatt GradIPM is a Personnel Management and Employment Consultant; her other books include *Recruiting Success* and *Jobhunt*, and she has contributed regularly to the press on employment matters.
128pp illus. 0 7463 0554 0.

How to Know Your Rights at Work
Robert Spicer MA

Written in clear English, this easy-to-follow handbook sets out everyone's rights at work whether in an office, shop, factory or other setting. It outlines the legal framework, the general duties of employers and employees, the legal scope of 'employment', confidential information, references, being a company director, the contract of employment, pay and deductions, hours of work, absences from work, disciplinary procedures, the ACAS code of practice, the meaning of 'gross misconduct', and grievance procedures.

'Justifiably described as a practical guide to employment law. It is clearly written in language readily understood by the layman... The text has been well laid out and sections are clearly signposted... The extensive use of case study material is interesting and helpful... The book is not only relevant to Careers Officers and their clients, but also to other people working in the employment/employment advisory field, eg. Citizens Advice Bureaux workers, personnel officers, Trade Union Personnel, and indeed anyone wishing to find out about their rights at work... The sort of book that can be easily dipped into for specific information, but which is interesting enough in its own right to be read from cover to cover.' *Careers Officer Journal.* 'Sets out in simple English everything an employee can expect in today's working environment.' *Kent Evening Post.*

Robert Spicer MA(Cantab) is a practising barrister, legal editor and author who specialises in employment law. He was Editor of the Case Index on Employment Law (Kluwer) and has taught law at Bristol University and Bristol Polytechnic.
131pp. 1 85703 009 5.

How to Master Business English
Michael Bennie

Are you communicating effectively? Do your business documents achieve the results you want? Or are they too often ignored or misunderstood? Good communication is the key to success in any business. Whether you are trying to sell a product, answer a query or complaint, or persuade colleagues, the way you express yourelf is often as important as what you say. With lots of examples, checklists and questionnaires to help you, this book will speed you on you way, whether as manager, executive, or business student. Contents: Introduction, communication in business, planning, getting the right reaction, the writing process, layout, letters, memos, reports, construction, style, sales letters, letters of complaint, answering complaints, accounts queries, press releases, reports, filing, grammar, punctuation, spelling, glossary, answers to exercises.

> 'An excellent book—not in the least dull... Altogether most useful for anyone seeking to improve their communication skills.' *IPS Journal.* 'Gives guidance on writing styles for every situation... steers the reader through the principles and techniques of effective letter-writing and document-planning.' *First Voice.* 'Useful chapters on grammar, punctuation and spelling. Frequent questionnaires and checklists enable the reader to check progress.' *Focus (Society of Business Teachers).*

Michael Bennie is a Director of Studies of the Department of Business Writing of Writers College, and author of *How to Do Your Own Advertising* in this series.
£7.99, 208pp illus. 0 7463 0582 6

How to Master Public Speaking
Anne Nicholls

Speaking well in public is one of the most useful skills any of us can acquire. People who can often become leaders in their business, profession or community, and the envy of their friends and colleagues. Whether you are a nervous novice or a practised pro, this step-by-step handbook tells you everything you need to know to master this highly prized communication skill. Contents: Preface, being a skilled communicator, preparation, researching your audience, preparing a speech, finding a voice, body language and non-verbal communication, dealing with nerves, audiovisual aids, the physical environment, putting it all together on the day, audience feedback, dealing with the media, glossary, further reading, useful contacts, index. Anne Hulbert Nicholls BA(Hons) PGCE was a Lecturer in Communications and Journalism in a College of Education for 14 years and ran courses in Presentation Skills and Effective Speaking for local business people. She now runs seminars and conferences for a publishing company and writes articles for a number of national magazines and newspapers. Her articles appear regularly in *Living* magazine. She has also worked in Public Relations and for BBC Radio.
160pp illus. 0 7563 0521 4.